Cambridge Certificate in Advanced English 1

WITHOUT ANSWERS

Official examination papers from University of Cambridge ESOL Examinations

CAMBRIDGE
UNIVERSITY PRESS

CAMBRIDGE UNIVERSITY PRESS
Cambridge, New York, Melbourne, Madrid, Cape Town, Singapore, São Paulo, Delhi

Cambridge University Press
The Edinburgh Building, Cambridge CB2 8RU, UK

www.cambridge.org
Information on this title: www.cambridge.org/9780521714419

First published 2008
Reprinted 2008

Printed in the United Kingdom at the University Press, Cambridge

A catalogue record for this publication is available from the British Library

ISBN 978-0-521-714419 Student's Book without answers
ISBN 978-0-521-714426 Student's Book with answers
ISBN 978-0-521-714457 CD (audio) set
ISBN 978-0-521-714433 Self-study Pack

Contents

Thanks and acknowledgements

The authors and publishers acknowledge the following sources of copyright material and are grateful for the permissions granted. While every effort has been made, it has not always been possible to identify the sources of all the material used, or to trace all copyright holders. If any omissions are brought to our notice, we will be happy to include the appropriate acknowledgements on reprinting.

Faber & Faber Limited, Greene & Heaton and Henry Holt & Co for the adapted text on p. 8: 'The Giordano Painting' from *Headlong* by Michael Frayn. Copyright © 1999 Michael Frayn. Reproduced by permission of Faber & Faber Limited, Greene & Heaton and Henry Holt & Co; *The Independent* for the adapted article on p. 10: 'When the hippos roar, start paddling!' by Richard Jackson, *The Independent* 10 February 1996. Copyright © Independent News & Media Limited; Telegraph Media Group for the adapted article on p. 12: 'The opera-lover turned crime novelist' by Michael White, *The Sunday Telegraph Review*, 23 March 2003; for the adapted article on p. 38: 'Fake art meets real money' by William Langley, *The Sunday Telegraph Review*, 29 June 2003; for the adapted article on p. 64: 'Lights, camera action man' by Richard Madden, *The Daily Telegraph*, 18 August 1998. Used by permission of Telegraph Media Group Limited; Jonathan Hancock for 'Picture this … with your mind's eye' on p. 15: from *Professional Manager*, July 1998. Used by permission of Jonathan Hancock; Taylor & Francis Books Ltd for the adapted extract on p. 33: 'How useful is the term "non-verbal expression?"' from *Communicating the Multiple Modes of Human Interconnection* by Ruth Finnegan. Copyright © 2002; and the extract 'A system to notate dance' on p. 61: from *Labanotation* by Ann Hutchinson Guest. Copyright © 2005; and the adapted article on p. 93: 'Over-consumption' by Paul Wachtel from *Political Ecology*. Used by permission of Taylor & Francis Books Ltd; NI Syndication for the adapted text on p. 36: 'Chocolate Cake Wars' by Chandos Elletson, *The Sunday Times*, 22 April 2000; and the adapted text on p. 90: 'Travelling sensitively' by Mark Hodson, *The Sunday Times Travel Magazine*, 16 February 1997. Copyright © NI Syndication. Used by permission of NI Syndication; Keith Wheatley for the text on p. 41: 'Offshore Vestments' from *The Financial Times, How to Spend it*, May 1998. Used by kind permission of Keith Wheatley; Cathy Marston for the adapted extract on p. 59: 'A choreographer's diary' from www.ballet.co.uk. Used by kind permission of Cathy Marston; Rupert Wright for the extract on p. 67: 'Mazes' from *The Financial Times, How to Spend it*, October 2001. Used by kind permission of Rupert Wright; Penguin Books Ltd for the adapted text on p. 87: 'Interviewing Londoners' from *My East End, A History of Cockney London* by Gilda O'Neill (Viking Books, 1999, 2000) Copyright Gilda O'Neill 1999, 2000. Reproduced by permission of Penguin Books Ltd; Simon de Burton for the text on p. 88: 'After the Frisbee' from *Weekend Financial Times Magazine, Issue 55*. Used by kind permission of Simon de Burton; Classic FM Magazine for the adapted text on p. 99: 'How music was written down' by Jeremy Nicholas from *Classic FM Magazine*, August 2004. Used with kind permission of Classic FM Magazine.

Colour section

Alamy/Alex Segre p. C8 (b); Alamy/Blickwinkel p. C7 (b); Alamy/Chris Stock p. C12 (bl); Alamy/David R Frazier Photography p. C2 (r); Alamy/F1 Online p. C9 (b); Alamy/Image State p. C12 (tl); Alamy/Jordi Cami p. C12 (tc); Alamy/Manfred Grebler p. C12 (tr); Aamy/Mark Gibson p. C4 (tr); Alamy/Peter Steiner p. C9 (tl); Alamy/Steve Skjold p. C12 (br); Corbis/Andanson James/Sygma p. C4 (b); Corbis/Barry Lewis p. C8 (tr); Corbis/Image 100 p. C1 (tr); Corbis/Kevin Fleming p. C2 (bl); Corbis/Macduff Everton p. C10 (b); Corbis/Paul Thompson p. C12 (cl); Corbis/Roy Rainford/Robert Harding World Imagery p. C9 (cl); Corbis/Tetra Images p. C7 (t); Daniel Goodchild/Photographers Direct p. C10 (tl); Getty Images/AFP p. C5 (bl); Getty Images/AFP p. C9 (c); Getty Images/Bongarts p. C1 (b); Getty Images/Lonely Planet p. C1 (tl); Getty Images/News p. C9 (tr); Getty Images/Photographers Choice p. C9 (cr); Getty Images/Photonica p. C7 (c); Getty Images/Science Faction p. C9 (br); Getty Images/Stone p. C8 (tl); Getty Images/Taxi p. C4 (tl); Getty Images/Taxi p. C5 (br); PA Photos p. C11 (b); Punchstock/Blend Images p. C10 (tr); Punchstock/Creatas p. C11 (tr); Punchstock/Goodshoot p. C5 (t); Roger Davies/Photographers Direct p. C11 (tl); Still Pictures/Iwao Yamamoto-UNEP p. C2 (tl); United States Geological Society p. C10 (inset).

Black and white section

Alamy/AM Corporation p. 63; Alamy/Foodfolio p. 36; Alamy/Skyscan Photolibrary p. 67; Science Photo Library/Chris Butler p. 70

Introduction

This collection of four complete practice tests comprises papers from the University of Cambridge ESOL Examinations Certificate in Advanced English (CAE) examination; students can practise these tests on their own or with the help of a teacher.

The CAE examination is part of a suite of general English examinations produced by Cambridge ESOL. This suite consists of five examinations that have similar characteristics but are designed for different levels of English language ability. Within the five levels, CAE is at Level C1 in the Council of Europe's *Common European Framework of Reference for Languages: Learning, teaching, assessment*. It has also been accredited by the Qualifications and Curriculum Authority in the UK as a Level 2 ESOL certificate in the National Qualifications Framework. The CAE examination is widely recognised in commerce and industry and in individual university faculties and other educational institutions.

Examination	Council of Europe Framework Level	UK National Qualifications Framework Level
CPE Certificate of Proficiency in English	C2	3
CAE Certificate in Advanced English	C1	2
FCE First Certificate in English	B2	1
PET Preliminary English Test	B1	Entry 3
KET Key English Test	A2	Entry 2

Further information

The information contained in this practice book is designed to be an overview of the exam. For a full description of all of the above exams including information about task types, testing focus and preparation, please see the relevant handbooks which can be obtained from Cambridge ESOL at the address below or from the website at: www.CambridgeESOL.org

University of Cambridge ESOL Examinations
1 Hills Road
Cambridge CB1 2EU
United Kingdom

Telephone: +44 1223 553997
Fax: +44 1223 553621
e-mail: ESOLHelpdesk@ucles.org.uk

The structure of CAE: an overview

The CAE examination consists of five papers.

Paper 1   Reading   1 hour 15 minutes
This paper consists of **four** parts, each containing one text or several shorter pieces. There are 34 questions in total, including multiple choice, gapped text and multiple matching.

Paper 2   Writing   1 hour 30 minutes
This paper consists of **two** parts which carry equal marks. In Part 1, which is **compulsory**, input material of up to 150 words is provided on which candidates have to base their answers. Candidates have to write either an article, a letter, a proposal, or a report of between 180 and 220 words.

  In Part 2, there are four tasks from which candidates **choose one** to write about. The range of tasks from which questions may be drawn includes an article, a competition entry, a contribution to a longer piece, an essay, an information sheet, a letter, a proposal, a report and a review. The last question is based on the set books. These books remain on the list for two years. Look on the website, or contact the Cambridge ESOL Local Secretary in your area for the up-to-date list of set books. The question on the set books has two options from which candidates **choose one** to write about. In this part, candidates have to write between 220 and 260 words.

Paper 3   Use of English   1 hour
This paper consists of **five** parts and tests control of English grammar and vocabulary. There are 50 questions in total. The tasks include gap-filling exercises, word formation, lexical appropriacy and sentence transformation.

Paper 4   Listening   40 minutes (approximately)
This paper consists of **four** parts. Each part contains a recorded text or texts and some questions including multiple choice, sentence completion and multiple matching. There is a total of 30 questions. Each text is heard twice.

Paper 5   Speaking   15 minutes
This paper consists of **four** parts. The standard test format is two candidates and two examiners. One examiner takes part in the conversation while the other examiner listens. Both examiners give marks. Candidates will be given photographs and other visual and written material to look at and talk about. Sometimes candidates will talk with the other candidates, sometimes with the examiner and sometimes with both.

Grading

The overall CAE grade is based on the total score gained in all five papers. Each paper is weighted to 40 marks. Therefore, the five CAE papers total 200 marks, after weighting. It is not necessary to achieve a satisfactory level in all five papers in order to pass the examination. Certificates are given to candidates who pass the examination with grade A, B or C. A is the highest. D and E are failing grades. All candidates are sent a Statement of Results which includes a graphical profile of their performance in each paper and shows their relative performance in each one.

  For further information on grading and results, go to the website (see page 5).

Test 1

PAPER 1   READING (1 hour 15 minutes)

Part 1

You are going to read three extracts which are all concerned in some way with providing a service. For questions **1–6**, choose the answer (**A**, **B**, **C** or **D**) which you think fits best according to the text. Mark your answers **on the separate answer sheet**.

Fish who work for a living

Cleaner wrasses are small marine fish that feed on the parasites living on the bodies of larger fish. Each cleaner owns a 'station' on a reef where clientele come to get their mouths and teeth cleaned. Client fish come in two varieties: residents and roamers. Residents belong to species with small territories; they have no choice but to go to their local cleaner. Roamers, on the other hand, either hold large territories or travel widely, which means that they have several cleaning stations to choose from. The cleaner wrasses sometimes 'cheat'. This occurs when the fish takes a bite out of its client, feeding on healthy mucus. This makes the client jolt and swim away.

Roamers are more likely to change stations if a cleaner has ignored them for too long or cheated them. Cleaners seem to know this: if a roamer and a resident arrive at the same time, the cleaner almost always services the roamer first. Residents can be kept waiting. The only category of fish that cleaners never cheat are predators, who possess a radical counterstrategy, which is to swallow the cleaner. With predators, cleaner fish wisely adopt an unconditionally cooperative strategy.

1   Which of the following statements about the cleaner wrasses is true?

    A   They regard 'roamer' fish as important clients.
    B   They take great care not to hurt any of their clients.
    C   They are too frightened to feed from the mouths of certain clients.
    D   They are in a strong position as they can move to find clients elsewhere.

2   The writer uses business terms in the text to

    A   illustrate how fish negotiate rewards.
    B   show how bigger fish can dominate smaller ones.
    C   exemplify cooperation in the animal world.
    D   describe the way fish take over a rival's territory.

Extract from a novel

The Giordano painting

'I was up in town yesterday,' I tell Tony easily, turning back from my long study of the sky outside the window as if I'd simply been wondering whether the matter was worth mentioning, 'and someone I was talking to thinks he knows someone who might possibly be interested.'

Tony frowns. 'Not a dealer?' he queries suspiciously.

'No, no – a collector. Said to be keen on seventeenth-century art. Especially the paintings of Giordano. *Very* keen.'

'Money all right?' Tony asks.

'Money, as I understand it, is far from being a problem.'

So, it's all happening. The words are coming. And it's not at all a bad start, it seems to me. I'm impressed with myself. I've given him a good spoonful *line 12* of jam to sweeten the tiny pill that's arriving next.

'Something of a mystery man, though, I gather,' I say solemnly. 'Keeps a low profile. Won't show his face in public.'

Tony looks at me thoughtfully. And sees right through me. All my boldness vanishes at once. I've been caught cheating my neighbours! I feel the panic rise.

'You mean he wouldn't want to come down here to look at it?'

'I don't know,' I flounder hopelessly. 'Perhaps . . . possibly . . .'

'Take it up to town,' he says decisively. 'Get your chum to show it to him.'

I'm too occupied in breathing again to be able to reply. He misconstrues my silence.

'Bit of a bore for you,' he says.

3   When he brings up the subject of the Giordano painting, the narrator wants to give Tony the impression of being

    A   cautious.
    B   resigned.
    C   mysterious.
    D   casual.

4   What is the narrator referring to when he uses the expression 'tiny pill' in line 12?

    A   his shortage of precise details about the collector
    B   his lack of certainty about the value of the painting
    C   his concerns about the collector's interest in the painting
    D   his doubts about the collector's ability to pay for the painting

The invention of banking

The invention of banking preceded that of coinage. Banking originated something like 4,000 years ago in Ancient Mesopotamia, in present-day Iraq, where the royal palaces and temples provided secure places for the safe-keeping of grain and other commodities. Receipts came to be used for transfers not only to the original depositors but also to third parties. Eventually private houses in Mesopotamia also got involved in these banking operations, and laws regulating them were included in the code of Hammurabi, the legal code developed not long afterwards.

In Ancient Egypt too, the centralisation of harvests in state warehouses led to the development of a system of banking. Written orders for the withdrawal of separate lots of grain by owners whose crops had been deposited there for safety and convenience, or which had been compulsorily deposited to the credit of the king, soon became used as a more general method of payment of debts to other people, including tax gatherers, priests and traders. Even after the introduction of coinage, these Egyptian grain banks served to reduce the need for precious metals, which tended to be reserved for foreign purchases, particularly in connection with military activities.

5   In both Mesopotamia and Egypt the banking systems

    A   were initially limited to transactions involving depositors.
    B   were created to provide income for the king.
    C   required a large staff to administer them.
    D   grew out of the provision of storage facilities for food.

6   What does the writer suggest about banking?

    A   It can take place without the existence of coins.
    B   It is likely to begin when people are in debt.
    C   It normally requires precious metals.
    D   It was started to provide the state with an income.

Part 2

You are going to read a magazine article about hippos. Six paragraphs have been removed from the article. Choose from the paragraphs **A–G** the one which fits each gap (**7–12**). There is one extra paragraph which you do not need to use. Mark your answers **on the separate answer sheet**.

When the hippos roar, start paddling!

Richard Jackson and his wife spent their honeymoon going down the Zambezi river in a canoe.

'They say this is a good test of a relationship,' said Tim as he handed me the paddle. I wasn't sure that such a tough challenge was what was needed on a honeymoon, but it was too late to go back. My wife, Leigh, and I were standing with our guide, Tim Came, on the banks of the Zambezi near the Zambia/Botswana border. This was to be the highlight of our honeymoon: a safari downriver, ending at the point where David Livingstone first saw the Victoria Falls.

| 7 | |

Neither of us had any canoeing experience. Tentatively we set off downstream, paddling with more enthusiasm than expertise. Soon we heard the first distant rumblings of what seemed like thunder. 'Is that Victoria Falls?' we inquired naïvely. 'No,' said Tim dismissively. 'That's our first rapid.' Easy, we thought. Wrong!

| 8 | |

The canoe plotted a crazed path as we careered from side to side, our best efforts seeming only to add to our plight. This was the first of many rapids, all relatively minor, all enjoyably challenging for tourists like us.

| 9 | |

The overnight stops would mean mooring at a deserted island in the middle of the river, where Tim's willing support team would be waiting, having erected a camp and got the water warm for our bucket showers. As the ice slowly melted in the drinks, restaurant-quality food would appear from a cooker using hot coals. Then people would begin to relax, and the day's stories would take on epic proportions.

| 10 | |

One morning, Tim decided to count the number of hippos we saw, in an attempt to gauge the population in this part of the river. Most of the wildlife keeps a cautious distance, and we were assured that, safe in our canoe, any potential threats would be more scared of us than we were of them – but we had been warned to give these river giants a wide berth. They'd normally stay in mid-stream, watching us with some suspicion, and greeting our departure with a cacophony of grunts.

| 11 | |

Tim yelled 'Paddle!' and over the next 100 metres an Olympic runner would have struggled to keep up with us. The hippo gave up the chase, and although Tim said he was just a youngster showing off, our opinion was that he had honeymooners on the menu. That would certainly be the way we told the story by the time we got home.

| 12 | |

At some times of the year, you can even enjoy a natural *jacuzzi* in one of the rock pools beside the falls. The travel brochures say it's the world's most exclusive picnic spot. It's certainly the ideal place to wind down after a near miss with a hippo.

A   Luckily we could make our mistakes in privacy as, apart from Tim and another couple, for two days we were alone. Our only other company was the array of bird and animal life. The paddling was fairly gentle, and when we got tired, Tim would lead us to the shore and open a cool-box containing a picnic lunch.

B   If that was the scariest moment, the most romantic was undoubtedly our final night's campsite. Livingstone Island is perched literally on top of Victoria Falls. The safari company we were with have exclusive access to it: it's just you, a sheer drop of a few hundred metres and the continual roar as millions of litres of water pour over the edge.

C   There was plenty of passing traffic to observe on land as well – giraffes, hippos, elephants and warthogs, while eagles soared overhead. We even spotted two rare white rhinos. We paddled closer to get a better look.

D   We had a four-metre aluminium canoe to ourselves. It was a small craft for such a mighty river, but quite big enough to house the odd domestic dispute. Couples had, it seemed, ended similar trips arguing rather than paddling. But it wasn't just newly-weds at risk. Tim assured us that a group of comedians from North America had failed to see the funny side too.

E   But number 150 had other ideas. As we hugged the bank he dropped under the water. We expected him to re-surface in the same spot, as the others had done. Instead, there was a sudden roar and he emerged lunging towards the canoe.

F   Over the next hour or so the noise grew to terrifying dimensions. By the time we edged around the bend to confront it, we were convinced we would be faced with mountains of white water. Instead, despite all the sound and fury, the Zambezi seemed only slightly ruffled by a line of small rocks.

G   When we'd all heard enough, we slept under canvas, right next to the river bank. Fortunately, we picked a time of year largely free of mosquitoes, so our nets and various lotions remained unused. The sounds of unseen animals were our nightly lullaby.

Part 3

You are going to read a newspaper article about a novelist. For questions **13–19**, choose the answer (**A**, **B**, **C** or **D**) which you think fits best according to the text. Mark your answers **on the separate answer sheet**.

The opera-lover turned crime novelist

Through her series of crime novels, Donna Leon has been solving murders in Venice with great panache – mostly to the soundtrack of grand opera.

Donna Leon first launched herself as a crime writer in 1991 with *Death at La Fenice*, which saw a conductor poisoned in mid-performance at the Venice opera house. 'It was an idea that kind of grew,' she says. 'I had a friend at the opera house. One day we were backstage, complaining about the tyrannical conductor – and we thought it would be a laugh to make him the victim in a crime novel, which I duly went off and wrote. But that's all it was meant to be. I was lucky to be born without ambition, and I had none for this book. Then I sent it off to a competition, and six months later they wrote back to say I'd won. I got a contract, and suddenly I had a purpose in life, a mission.'

To hear her talk, you'd think that until *Death at La Fenice* she'd been living in obscurity. Not so. She was a well-known academic teaching English literature at universities in the USA and Europe. But she found that she wasn't really cut out for university life, and finally decided to walk out on it. 'I'm a former academic,' she says now through slightly gritted teeth. And it's interesting that her literary reputation has been made through a medium so remote from the one she used to teach.

'You'd be surprised how many academics do read murder mystery though,' she adds. 'It makes no intellectual demands, and it's what you want after a day of literary debate.' That said, Ms Leon is big business. She sells in bulk, her books are translated into nineteen languages and she's a household name in German-speaking countries. 'All of which is gratifying for me personally, and I don't mean to rubbish my own work, but murder mystery is a craft, not an art. Some people go to crime conventions and deliver learned papers on the way Agatha Christie presents her characters, but they're out of their minds. I stay away from such events.'

Leon also stays away from most of the other expected haunts of crime writers, like courtrooms and police stations – 'I've only known two policemen, neither of them well,' – which accounts for the absence of technical legal detail in the books. What's more, the few points of police procedure that appear are usually invented – as, she admits, they're bound to be when you set a murder series in a place where murders never happen. 'Venice is small, compact, protected by its geography – there's really not much crime.' Clearly

the key thing about her murder stories isn't credibility. Predictability comes closer to the mark: setting a series in a fixed location that the reader finds attractive, with a constant cast of characters.

And that's what Donna Leon does. Her unique selling point is Venice which, as the reviewers always say, comes through with such vitality and forcefulness in Leon's writing that you can smell it. There's a set cast of characters, led by a middle-aged detective, Commissario Brunetti, and his wife (a disillusioned academic). Then there are her standard jokes – often to do with food. Indeed, Leon lingers so ecstatically over the details of lunch, the pursuit of justice frequently gets diverted. The eating is a literary device – part of the pattern of each novel, into which she slots the plot. 'That's how you hook your readers, who like a kind of certainty. And the most attractive certainty of crime fiction is that it gives them what real life doesn't. The bad guy gets it in the end.'

Indeed, when the conversation switches to Donna Leon's other life, *Il Complesso Barocco*, the opera company she helps run, she talks about baroque opera as though it were murder-mystery: fuelled by 'power, jealousy and rage, despair, menace' which are her own words for the sleeve notes of a new CD of Handel arias by the company, packaged under the title *The Abandoned Sorceress*. Designed to tour rare works in concert format, *Il Complesso* was set up in 2001 in collaboration with another US exile in Italy, the musicologist Alan Curtis. 'It started as a one-off. There was a rare Handel opera, *Arminio*, that Alan thought should be performed, and it became an obsession for him until eventually I said, 'Do you want to talk about this or do you want to do it?' So we did it. I rang a friend who runs a Swiss opera festival. We offered him a production. Then had eight months to get it together.'

Somehow it came together, and *Il Complesso* is now an ongoing venture. Curtis does the hands-on artistic and administrative work. Leon lends her name which 'opens doors in all those German-speaking places' and, crucially, underwrites the costs. In addition, her publishing commitments take her all over Europe – where she keeps a lookout for potential singers, and sometimes even features in the productions herself: not singing ('I don't') but reading the odd snatch from her books.

13 What is suggested about the novel *Death at La Fenice* in the first paragraph?

    A Donna based the plot on a real-life event she had witnessed.

    B Donna didn't envisage the work ever being taken very seriously.

    C Donna had to be persuaded that it was good enough to win a prize.

    D Donna embarked upon it as a way of bringing about a change in her life.

14 The second paragraph paints a picture of Donna as someone who

    A has little respect for her fellow academics.

    B regrets having given up her job in a university.

    C was unsuited to being a university teacher.

    D failed to make a success of her academic career.

15 From Donna's comments in the third paragraph, we understand that

    A she feels crime fiction should be considered alongside other types of literature.

    B she is pleased with the level of recognition that her own novels have received.

    C she regards her own novels as inferior to those of Agatha Christie.

    D she finds the popularity of crime novels amongst academics very satisfying.

16 Donna is described as an untypical crime writer because

    A she is able to imagine crimes being committed by unlikely characters.

    B she is unconcerned whether or not her stories appear realistic.

    C she has little interest in the ways criminals think and operate.

    D she manages to come up with imaginative new ideas for her plots.

17 Donna's greatest strength as a crime writer is seen as

    A her avoidance of a fixed approach.

    B her injection of humour into her stories.

    C the clear moral message she puts across.

    D the strong evocation of place she achieves.

18 When Donna helped set up *Il Complesso Barocco,*

    A she didn't expect it to be a long-term project.

    B she saw it as more interesting than her writing work.

    C she had a fundamental disagreement with her main collaborator.

    D she was attracted by the challenge of the first deadline.

19 In what way is Donna important to *Il Complesso Barocco?*

    A She provides essential financial support.

    B She oversees its day-to-day organisation.

    C She helps as a translator.

    D She organises the recruitment of performers.

Part 4

You are going to read an article about the human mind. For questions **20–34,** choose from the sections (**A–E**). The sections may be chosen more than once.

Mark your answers **on the separate answer sheet**.

Which section mentions the following?

things that you will not need if you adopt a certain mental technique	20
using an image of a familiar place to help you remember things	21
being able to think about both particular points and general points	22
things that you may not have a clear mental picture of	23
something which appears to be disorganised	24
annoyance at your inability to remember things	25
bearing in mind what you want to achieve in the future	26
an example of an industry in which people use pictures effectively	27
an everyday example of failure to keep information in the mind	28
the impact a certain mental technique can have on people listening to what you say	29
an assertion that certain things can be kept in your mind more easily than others	30
information that it is essential to recall in certain situations	31
being able to consider things from various points of view	32
things that come into your mind in an illogical sequence	33
remembering written work by imagining it in context	34

Picture this ... with your mind's eye

Trying to understand and cope with life, we impose our own frameworks on it and represent information in different symbolic forms in our mind, writes Jonathan Hancock.

A

Think of the mental maps you use to find your way around the places you live and work. Which way up do you picture towns and cities you know well? Which details are highlighted, which ones blurred? Just as the map of London used by passengers on the Underground is different from the one used by drivers above ground, so your mental framework differs from that of other people. We also use frameworks to organise more abstract information. Many people say that they can visualise the position of key passages in books or documents. Mention a point made by the author, and they can recall and respond to it by picturing it in relation to other key points within the larger framework they see in their mind's eye. On a chaotic-looking desk, it is often possible to see a mental picture of where the key pieces of paper are and find a particular document in seconds.

B

We all have our own natural strategies for structuring information, for altering and re-arranging it in our mind's eye. You can take control of your thinking by increasing your control of the mental frameworks you create. Since Ancient Roman times, a specific framing technique has been used to improve memory and boost clarity of thought. The concept is simple: you design an empty framework, based on the shape of a building you know well, and get used to moving around its rooms and hallways in your mind. Whenever you have information to remember, you place it in this 'virtual storehouse'. Whatever it is you are learning – words, numbers, names, jobs, ideas – you invent pictorial clues to represent each one. The mind prefers images to abstract ideas, and can retain vast numbers of visual clues. Just as advertisers bring concepts to life with key images, you highlight the important points in a batch of information and assign each of them an illustration.

C

Memory and place are closely linked. Have you ever walked upstairs, forgotten what you went for, but remembered when you returned to where you were standing when you first had the thought? When you are trying to learn new information, it makes sense to use the mind's natural tendencies. In your mind, you return to the imaginary rooms in your 'virtual storehouse', and rediscover the images you left there. Cicero, perhaps the greatest orator in history, is reputed to have used this technique to recall complex legal arguments, addressing the Roman Senate from memory for days on end. You can use it to remember all the employees in your new workplace, the jobs you have to do in a day, month or year, subject headings for a complex piece of work, or the facts you need to have at your fingertips under pressurised circumstances.

D

The system of combining images and ideas works so well because it involves 'global thinking', bringing together the two 'sides' of your brain. The left side governs logic, words, numbers, patterns and structured thought – the frameworks you build – and the right side works on random thoughts, pictures, daydreams – the memorable imagery you fill them with. The fearless, imaginative creativity of the child combines with the patterning, prioritising, structured thinking of the adult. The memory is activated with colours and feelings, as you create weird, funny, exciting, surreal scenes; and the information is kept under control by the organised frameworks you design. Imagination is the key. You enter a new dimension, dealing with information in a form that suits the way the mind works. In this accessible form, huge amounts of data can be carried around with you. You never again have to search around for an address book, diary or telephone number on a scrap of paper. Your memory becomes a key part of your success, rather than the thing you curse as the cause of your failure.

E

Bringing information into the field of your imagination helps you to explore it in greater depth and from different angles. Storing it in the frameworks of your mind allows you to pick out key details but also to see the big picture. You can use your trained memory to organise your life: to see the day-to-day facts and figures, names, times and dates, but also to keep in touch with your long-term goals. By understanding the way your mind works, you can make yourself memorable to others. Give your thoughts a shape and structure that can be grasped and others will remember what you have to say. You can take your imaginative grasp of the world to a new level and, by making the most of mental frames, you can put the information you need at your disposal more readily.

PAPER 2   WRITING (1 hour 30 minutes)

Part 1

You **must** answer this question. Write your answer in **180–220** words in an appropriate style.

---

1   You are studying at a college in Canada. Recently you and some other students attended a two-day Careers Conference. As the college paid for you, the College Principal has asked you to write a report about the conference. You and the other students have discussed the conference and you have made notes on their views.

Read the conference programme together with your notes below. Then, **using the information appropriately**, write a report for the Principal explaining how useful the conference was and making recommendations for next year.

CAREERS CONFERENCE

Vancouver Hall
Friday – Sunday, 9am–6pm
Exhibition – over 100 different jobs
Talks on wide range of careers
Experts available to give advice

Notes on students' views:

– **exhibition great**

– **some talks good**

– **not enough people to answer questions**

– **better for science students than e.g. language or history students**

Now write your **report** for the College Principal, as outlined above. You should use your own words as far as possible.

Part 2

Choose **one** of the following writing tasks. Your answer should follow exactly the instructions given. Write approximately **220–260** words.

2   You have seen the following announcement in an international magazine.

> # FASHION AND CHANGING LIFESTYLES
>
> Do you think that fashion reflects changes in how people live? We would like to know how fashion in clothes has changed since your grandparents were young, and what this reveals about changes in society in your country.
>
> The most interesting articles will be published in the next issue of our magazine.

Write your **article**.

3   An English-speaking friend is writing a book on TV programmes in different countries. Your friend has asked you for a contribution about the most popular TV programme in your country. Your contribution should:

- briefly describe the most popular TV programme
- explain why the programme is so popular
- explain whether or not you think it deserves its popularity.

Write your **contribution** to the book.

4   You see this notice in the local library of the town where you are studying English.

> The *International Development Agency* has given our town a grant to be spent on improving transport and housing facilities.
>
> The Planning Director invites you to send a proposal outlining any problems with existing transport **and** housing facilities and explaining how they can be improved. A decision can then be made about how the money should be spent.

Write your **proposal**.

5   Answer **one** of the following two questions based on **one** of the titles below.

(a) Kingsley Amis: *Lucky Jim*

As part of your course, your teacher has asked you for suggestions for a story to study in class. You decide to write about *Lucky Jim*. In your report, briefly outline the plot and say why you think *Lucky Jim* would be interesting for other students.

Write your **report**.

(b) John Grisham: *The Pelican Brief*

As part of your course you have chosen to write an essay with the following title.

'Who is the most corrupt character in *The Pelican Brief*? Give reasons for your views.'

Write your **essay**.

PAPER 3   USE OF ENGLISH (1 hour)

Part 1

For questions **1–12**, read the text below and decide which answer (**A, B, C** or **D**) best fits each gap. There is an example at the beginning (**0**).

Mark your answers **on the separate answer sheet**.

Example:

0 A instruction   **B** information   **C** opinion   **D** advice

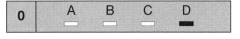

Girls and technology

If you want your daughter to succeed, buy her a toy construction set. That is the **(0)** ..... from Britain's **(1)** ..... female engineers and scientists. Marie-Noelle Barton, who heads an Engineering Council campaign to encourage girls into science and engineering, maintains that some of Britain's most successful women have had their careers **(2)** ..... by the toys they played with as children. Even girls who end **(3)** ..... nowhere near a microchip or microscope could benefit from a better **(4)** ..... of science and technology.

'It's a **(5)** ..... of giving them experience and confidence with technology so that when they are **(6)** ..... with a situation requiring some technical know-how, they feel they can handle it and don't just **(7)** ..... defeat immediately,' says Mrs Barton. 'I believe that lots of girls feel unsure of themselves when it comes **(8)** ..... technology and therefore they might be losing out on jobs because they are reluctant even to apply for them.'

Research recently carried **(9)** ..... suggests that scientific and constructional toys should be **(10)** ..... to girls from an early age, otherwise the result is 'socialisation' into stereotypically female **(11)** ..... , which may explain why relatively few girls study science and engineering at university in Britain. Only 14% of those who have gone for engineering **(12)** ..... at university this year are women, although this figure does represent an improvement on the 7% recorded some years ago.

---

1 **A** foremost   **B** uppermost   **C** predominant   **D** surpassing

2 **A** styled   **B** shaped   **C** built   **D** modelled

3 **A** in   **B** by   **C** on   **D** up

4 **A** hold   **B** grasp   **C** insight   **D** realisation

5 **A** matter   **B** situation   **C** state   **D** cause

6 **A** approached   **B** encountered   **C** presented   **D** offered

7 **A** admit   **B** allow   **C** receive   **D** permit

8 **A** for   **B** to   **C** from   **D** with

9 **A** off   **B** through   **C** forward   **D** out

10 **A** accessible   **B** feasible   **C** reachable   **D** obtainable

11 **A** characters   **B** parts   **C** states   **D** roles

12 **A** options   **B** alternatives   **C** selections   **D** preferences

Part 2

For questions **13–27**, read the text below and think of the word which best fits each gap. Use only **one** word in each gap. There is an example at the beginning **(0)**.

Write your answers **IN CAPITAL LETTERS on the separate answer sheet.**

Example: | 0 | W | I | T | H | | | | | | | | | | | | | | |

Weather in Antarctica

The most extreme weather conditions experienced in Antarctica are associated **(0)** ….. blizzards. These are simply strong winds with falling snow **(13)** ….. , more commonly, snow that is picked up and pushed along the ground by the wind. Blizzards may last for days at **(14)** ….. time, and in some cases it can be almost impossible for people to see. It is not unusual **(15)** ….. objects only about a metre or **(16)** ….. away to become unrecognisable. Scientists doing research in the area **(17)** ….. then confined to their tents or caravans. We think of blizzards **(18)** ….. extremely cold, while in fact temperatures in the Antarctic are usually higher than normal **(19)** ….. a blizzard. Major blizzards of several days in length occur more frequently in some locations than in others. **(20)** ….. may be eight or ten such blizzards in any particular place **(21)** ….. an annual basis. They often cause considerable damage, so that any scientific buildings or equipment constructed in this region must be specially made to give as **(22)** ….. protection as possible.

If the weather is fine, visibility in Antarctica is usually excellent because of the clear air and the absence of dust and smoke. **(23)** ….. this means is that people often greatly underestimate the distance of objects and features of the landscape. Also, very large features **(24)** ….. as mountains may appear to be above the horizon, or even upside **(25)** ….. . These 'mirages', **(26)** ….. are just tricks played by the eyes in certain conditions, have led to explorers in the Antarctic making many errors **(27)** ….. judgement.

Part 3

For questions **28–37**, read the text below. Use the word given in capitals at the end of some of the lines to form a word that fits in the gap **in the same line**. There is an example at the beginning **(0)**.

Write your answers **IN CAPITAL LETTERS on the separate answer sheet**.

Example: | **0** | F | O | U | N | D | E | R | | | | | | | | | | |

Freud and Dreams

Sigmund Freud is regarded as the **(0)** ..... of psychoanalysis. His work	**FOUND**
has been **(28)** ..... in many areas but he is perhaps best known for	**INFLUENCE**
having drawn our **(29)** ..... to dreams, which he believed were clues to inner	**ATTEND**
conflicts. The fact that a dream is **(30)** ..... a disguised expression of what is	**ESSENTIAL**
happening in the unconscious mind means that it is difficult for the dreamer	
to understand its **(31)** ..... . Freud believed that the sleeping mind resorted	**SIGNIFY**
to a whole range of unconscious wishes in forms which would prevent	
the dreamer from having any **(32)** ..... of their true nature. In Freud's	**AWARE**
view, interpreting the meaning of the dream required a psychoanalyst with	
an expert **(33)** ..... of how dreams disguise desires. The psychoanalyst's	**KNOW**
lack of personal **(34)** ..... in the dream would enable him to see the dream	**INVOLVE**
objectively.	
According to Freud, dreams use a **(35)** ..... symbolic language quite	**MYSTERY**
different from that of waking life, but the fact is there is no hard	
(36) ..... for believing that dreams really do reflect our unconscious wishes.	**EVIDENT**
Nevertheless, Freud **(37)** ..... made a major contribution to twentieth-century	**DOUBT**
thought and many useful insights into psychological processes have been	
gained through his work.	

Part 4

For questions **38–42**, think of **one** word only which can be used appropriately in all three sentences. Here is an example **(0)**.

Example:

0 The committee decided to .... the money equally between the two charities.

I can't believe that John and Maggie have decided to .... up after 20 years of marriage.

To serve a watermelon you need to .... it down the centre with a sharp knife.

Example: | **0** | S | P | L | I | T | | | | | | | | | | | | | |

Write **only** the missing word **IN CAPITAL LETTERS on the separate answer sheet**.

---

38 Sally's front tooth is very .... – I'm sure it'll come out soon.

Jane has lost so much weight that all her clothes are too ....

The horse got .... from the stable and started trotting towards the road.

39 The thief .... the watch into his pocket when he thought no one was looking.

Several visitors to the castle almost .... on the newly polished floor.

The speaker .... a few references to the local football team into his speech, which the audience appreciated greatly.

40 Chris arrived very early for his flight in order to be at the .... of the queue when the check-in desk opened.

My sister's got a really good .... for figures, but I'm hopeless at maths.

George has just been promoted to .... of department so he'll be even more busy from now on.

41 The restaurant .... out of fish quite early on in the evening.

The boat .... into a storm as it neared the French coast.

Mrs Benson .... the company single-handed after her husband's death.

42 This is the exact .... where the famous scene from the film was shot.

When they felt the first .... of rain, they gathered the picnic together and rushed inside.

The high .... of my trip around India was definitely the trip to Calcutta.

Part 5

For questions **43–50**, complete the second sentence so that it has a similar meaning to the first sentence, using the word given. **Do not change the word given.** You must use between **three** and **six** words, including the word given. Here is an example **(0)**.

Example:

0 Fernanda refused to wear her sister's old dress.

   NOT

   Fernanda said that .... her sister's old dress.

The gap can be filled with the words 'she would not wear', so you write:

Example: | **0** | SHE WOULD NOT WEAR |

Write the missing words **IN CAPITAL LETTERS on the separate answer sheet**.

_____

43 Mauro says he prefers to do his homework on his own.

   RATHER

   Mauro says that .... do his homework with other people.

44 Clara said that she had not seen the missing letter.

   HAVING

   Clara .... the missing letter.

45 It took Layla five minutes to find her car keys.

   SPENT

   Layla .... for her car keys.

46 A short meeting of the cast will take place after today's rehearsal.

BY

Today's rehearsal .... a short meeting of the cast.

47 I'll be happy to show you round the sights of my city when you come to visit me.

TAKE

It will be a .... sightseeing tour of my city when you come to visit me.

48 Rousseau painted fabulous pictures of the rainforest although he had never travelled outside Europe.

SPITE

Rousseau painted fabulous pictures of the rainforest .... travelled outside Europe.

49 It is thought that one in every five people cannot control how much they spend.

UNABLE

One in every five people is thought .... their spending under control.

50 My passport needs renewing because I'm going abroad this summer.

GET

I need .... because I'm going abroad this summer.

PAPER 4 LISTENING (approximately 40 minutes)

Part 1

You will hear three different extracts. For questions **1–6**, choose the answer (**A**, **B** or **C**) which fits best according to what you hear. There are two questions for each extract.

Extract One

You hear part of an interview with a woman who works in retail management.

1 How does the woman feel now about her first job in retailing?

   A pleased by the way she handled the staff

   B confident that it gave her a good start

   C relaxed about the mistakes she made

2 What is the woman advised to do next?

   A reflect on her skills

   B volunteer for extra work

   C discuss her situation with her boss

Extract Two

You overhear a woman telling a friend a story about a swan.

3 What problem did the woman have with the swan?

   A She misunderstood its intentions.

   B She underestimated the speed of its approach.

   C She failed to realise the consequences of disturbing it.

4 What is the man's reaction to the story?

   A He feels he would have handled the situation better.

   B He is unconvinced by the woman's version of events.

   C He fails to see quite how serious the problem was.

Extract Three

You hear part of an interview with Bruce Loader, a successful businessman who is talking about his early life.

5   Why did Bruce decide to give up the idea of studying art?

    A   He failed to gain a place at art college.

    B   He became tired of doing representational art.

    C   He was persuaded that he could not realise his ambition.

6   What was his father's reaction to Bruce's decision?

    A   He was anxious to discuss alternative employment options.

    B   He was angry that a good opportunity had been wasted.

    C   He was dismissive of the advantages of higher education.

Part 2

You will hear an explorer called Richard Livingstone talking about a trip he made in the rainforest of South America. For questions **7–14**, complete the sentences.

A Trip in the Rainforest

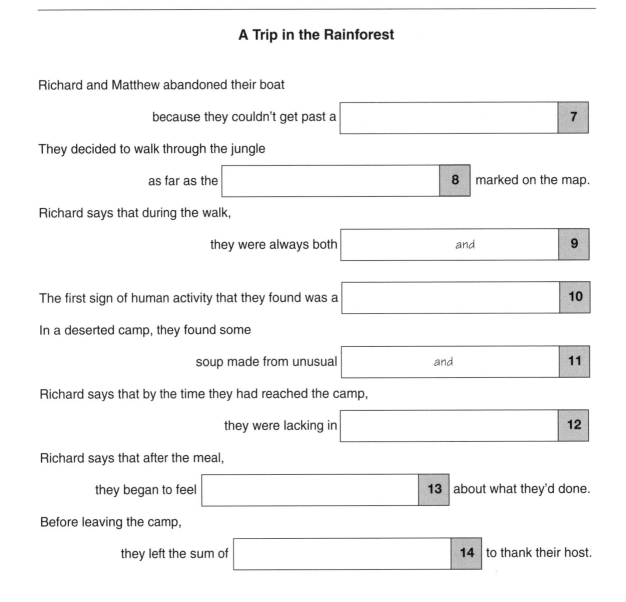

Richard and Matthew abandoned their boat

because they couldn't get past a | **7**

They decided to walk through the jungle

as far as the | **8** | marked on the map.

Richard says that during the walk,

they were always both | *and* | **9**

The first sign of human activity that they found was a | **10**

In a deserted camp, they found some

soup made from unusual | *and* | **11**

Richard says that by the time they had reached the camp,

they were lacking in | **12**

Richard says that after the meal,

they began to feel | **13** | about what they'd done.

Before leaving the camp,

they left the sum of | **14** | to thank their host.

Part 3

You will hear part of an interview with the astronaut Charles Duke, who is talking about his trip to the moon. For questions **15–20**, choose the answer (**A, B, C** or **D**) which fits best according to what you hear.

15   How did Charles feel about space travel as a boy?

    A   He thought it was unlikely to happen.
    B   He regarded it as more than science fiction.
    C   He was fascinated by the idea of it.
    D   He showed no particular interest in it.

16   What did Charles consider to be the hardest part of the training?

    A   feeling trapped in the heavy spacesuit
    B   endlessly practising the lunar surface landing
    C   constantly being afraid of making a mistake
    D   being unable to move his arms and hands

17   What was Charles's reaction when he first found out he was going to the moon?

    A   He realised he had to be cautious.
    B   He felt proud to be given the opportunity.
    C   He tried to control his excitement.
    D   He reflected on his chances of survival.

18   How did the crew feel when they had landed on the moon?

    A   They felt as if they were coming home.
    B   They realised they had achieved something special.
    C   They were afraid of what they might find on the surface.
    D   They were worried about how they would take off again.

19   What feature of the moon made the greatest impact on Charles?

    A   the brightness of the sun
    B   the vastness of the sky
    C   the loneliness of the place
    D   the absence of any stars

20   What does Charles feel was the most memorable part of his mission?

    A   nearly falling into a crater
    B   walking on the moon's surface
    C   seeing things never seen before
    D   holding a piece of the moon

Part 4

You will hear five short extracts in which people are talking about an occasion when they came into contact with a well-known celebrity.

TASK ONE

For questions **21–25**, choose from the list **A–H** what each speaker says about coming into contact with a celebrity.

TASK TWO

For questions **26–30**, choose from the list **A–H** the opinion each speaker gives about the celebrity.

While you listen you must complete both tasks.

TASK ONE		TASK TWO	
A I failed to recognise the person.		**A** He/She became more agitated than necessary.	
B I realised I had forgotten something.		**B** He/She enjoyed causing trouble.	
C I insisted on something.		**C** He/She appeared totally at ease.	
D I was upset by personal criticism.		**D** He/She expected too much privacy.	
E I had been given incorrect information.		**E** He/She seemed insincere.	
F I was pleasantly surprised.		**F** He/She wasn't able to cope with fame.	
G I refused a request.		**G** He/She talked down to me.	
H I was amused by something.		**H** He/She eventually accepted the regulations.	

Speaker 1	**21**	Speaker 1	**26**
Speaker 2	**22**	Speaker 2	**27**
Speaker 3	**23**	Speaker 3	**28**
Speaker 4	**24**	Speaker 4	**29**
Speaker 5	**25**	Speaker 5	**30**

PAPER 5   SPEAKING (15 minutes)

There are two examiners. One (the interlocutor) conducts the test, providing you with the necessary materials and explaining what you have to do. The other examiner (the assessor) is introduced to you, but then takes no further part in the interaction.

Part 1 (3 minutes)

The interlocutor first asks you and your partner a few questions. The interlocutor asks candidates for some information about themselves, then widens the scope of the questions by asking about, e.g. candidates' leisure activities, studies, travel and daily life. Candidates are expected to respond to the interlocutor's questions, and listen to what their partner has to say.

Part 2 (a one-minute 'long turn' for each candidate, plus 30-second response from the second candidate)

You are each given the opportunity to talk for about a minute, and to comment briefly after your partner has spoken.

The interlocutor gives you a set of pictures and asks you to talk about them for about one minute. It is important to listen carefully to the interlocutor's instructions. The interlocutor then asks your partner a question about your pictures and your partner responds briefly.

You are then given another set of pictures to look at. Your partner talks about these pictures for about one minute. This time the interlocutor asks you a question about your partner's pictures and you respond briefly.

Part 3 (approximately 4 minutes)

In this part of the test you and your partner are asked to talk together. The interlocutor places a new set of pictures on the table between you. This stimulus provides the basis for a discussion. The interlocutor explains what you have to do.

Part 4 (approximately 4 minutes)

The interlocutor asks some further questions, which leads to a more general discussion of what you have talked about in Part 3. You may comment on your partner's answers if you wish.

Test 2

PAPER 1   READING (1 hour 15 minutes)

Part 1

You are going to read three extracts which are all concerned in some way with communication. For questions **1–6**, choose the answer (**A**, **B**, **C** or **D**) which you think fits best according to the text. Mark your answers **on the separate answer sheet**.

How useful is the term 'non–verbal expression'?

The term 'non-verbal' is commonly used to describe such communicative resources as gesture, facial movement and tone of voice. The term has long been useful in challenging the misconception that words constitute the whole of communication. However, a further assumption has sometimes seemed to follow: that 'non-verbal' expression is something unitary, independent of verbal communicating, or classifiable under some single term like 'body language'. This is to drastically simplify our actual practice. As pointed out by writers on language and social interaction, gestural and vocal actions are often integrated rather than autonomous, and verbal and non-verbal communicating usually produced in a highly coordinated fashion. Proposing a concept of 'non-verbal expression' has led to an unfounded generalisation about this supposedly distinct subject: that it is the medium for expressing emotions and relations rather than conscious thought or ideas, for example. Even if this were true, the fact remains that the resources covered by the term 'non-verbal' are diverse and complex in the extreme. It can only be misleading to bunch them together as a distinctive communicative mode.

1   The writer supports the view that non-verbal expression

    A   is more complex than verbal expression.
    B   is a separate field of study from verbal expression.
    C   is commonly used in conjunction with verbal expression.
    D   is able to communicate more information than verbal expression.

2   The writer suggests that we should

    A   recognise the differences between verbal and non-verbal expression.
    B   be aware of the many aspects of non-verbal expression.
    C   do further research into non-verbal expression.
    D   accept the limitations of non-verbal expression.

Public speaking

Last year I started work with a new company. Unfortunately, in my new role I was required to speak in public, at conferences. The thought filled me with dread, because I was sure my voice was boring. Also, I wouldn't know what to say. Anyway, when the time came I tried not to panic, and went back to first principles: I made a plan, first deciding my key message. This gave me a structure, and was the first step to dispelling my nerves.

Then I found a voice coach who taught me how to relax and breathe properly. Suddenly there was power behind my voice and I found I was in control. It was like going to a vocal gym. Instead of gabbling my sentences, I slowed down and took time to enjoy the words.

I lacked the confidence at first to speak without a script, but I learnt not to write everything down to the last word – the audience switched off when I did that. A friend gave me the tip of memorising the first few sentences, then I could make eye contact with the people I was speaking to – engage with them.

3   In this article the writer's aim is to show that

    A public speaking need not be anything to worry about.
    B there is always something new for a speaker to learn.
    C it is important for a speaker to have an outgoing personality.
    D success in public speaking depends on the quality of the speaker's memory.

4   The writer says he trained in how to speak at conferences by

    A studying articles written by well-known public speakers.
    B attending a course on how to give effective presentations.
    C getting help with the physical aspects of public speaking.
    D following colleagues' advice on ways of keeping the audience's attention.

Iowa State University: Business and Technical Communication

Essay Assignment

This assignment asks you to write an essay suitable for publication in a professional journal or newsletter. You will identify an issue that's interesting to teachers and/or workplace professionals in business and technical communication and then pose a question you want to explore about that issue. Your essay will be an argument for a clearly stated position and should be presented in a logical, understandable, and engaging manner. Your essay should be targeted to a particular journal, which means that you need to read enough articles and essays in that journal to identify their general features.

Consider the following questions:

- What are the conventions of essays in the journal or newsletter you are targeting?
- What is the question you are addressing?
- What is the argument you are making?

Cover Memo

When you submit your essay, please include a cover sheet in which you identify the features of essay conventions that you consciously employed to make the essay appropriate for the intended journal or newsletter. This is the meta-cognitive element – you knowing not only what you've done but why you did it. Please indicate the journal or newsletter to which you plan to submit your revised essay.

5   What are students expected to do in their assignment?

   A   put forward an original idea about a subject
   B   provide support for a particular point of view on a topic
   C   present an argument against an existing essay or article
   D   offer a solution to an unresolved issue in a particular field

6   Along with their essay, students are asked to provide a note which

   A   indicates the reason for their choice of topic.
   B   identifies the background texts they have read.
   C   justifies their choice of intended journal or newsletter.
   D   specifies the essay-writing characteristics used in their assignment.

Part 2

You are going to read a newspaper article about chocolate cake. Six paragraphs have been removed from the article. Choose from the paragraphs **A–G** the one which fits each gap (**7–12**). There is one extra paragraph which you do not need to use. Mark your answers **on the separate answer sheet**.

CHOCOLATE CAKE WARS

It's the most imitated cake in the world. But who created the original Sacher torte, asks Chandos Elletson?

Vienna is heaven for cake lovers. After seeing the city's sights, there is nothing better to do than sit in a coffee house and gorge on delicious cakes. These great cakes, or *tortes*, are part of Austrian folklore, and the recipes for them are closely-guarded secrets. They were invented by brilliant and creative young chefs back in the mists of time and some have even been the subject of court cases between rival confectioners. Now, inevitably, the top Viennese cakes are even available over the internet.

7	

The date was 1832. In a royal palace outside Vienna, the Prince had sent an edict to the kitchen for a new dessert to be created in honour of some influential guests, and was anticipating something special. The head chef was ill and the order ended up with a 16-year-old pastry apprentice named Franz Sacher.

8	

What the chef thought when he returned is unknown, but Sacher kept his recipe a secret and named the cake after himself. He went on to found his own famous hotel and café. Today, hundreds of thousands of hungry customers, most of them tourists, come each year to eat the same cake, baked to its original recipe.

9	

Demel, founded in 1793, was one such business. Demel himself, who was baker and confectioner for the Emperor's palace, claimed that Sacher worked for him and that their Sacher torte was the true original. A court of law decided otherwise, and only Sacher may call the cake original. The Demel Sacher torte, as it is now known, differs minutely from the Sacher, but both cakes are made with secret blends of home-made chocolate.

10	

One contender is the Imperial Hotel in Vienna, whose Imperial torte is also sold online, and has a myth and a chef to go with it. This time it is 1873, and Emperor Franz Josef is about to inaugurate the Imperial and Royal Court Hotel. Junior cook Xavier Loibner wishes he could bake a cake for his Emperor like all the magnificent creations donated by the monarchy's top chefs.

11	

Judging by the date, the milk chocolate would also have been a first. According to *Chocolate: The Definitive Guide*, milk chocolate was not invented until 1875, when a Swiss confectioner mixed chocolate with the condensed milk made by his friend Henri Nestlé. Whatever the origin of the story, it is said that the Emperor noticed the unusually-shaped cake. He tried it, went back for more, and so the legend of the Imperial torte was born.

Now Loibner's recipe, a secret in keeping with Viennese tradition, has recently been rediscovered and, deep in the recesses of the hotel, a dedicated production kitchen churns out thousands of these delicate cakes for dispatch all over the world.

12	

So the chocolate cake wars are set to continue well into the twenty-first century. Only time will tell who wins the next round of the battle. In the meantime there is plenty of opportunity to test the market.

A However, a number of rivals strongly contended that their own version of the famous cake was actually the original. As a result, a chocolate cake war raged in Vienna's coffee houses for many years.

B The most famous and most imitated of all Viennese cakes is the Sacher torte. Its recipe is still secret despite a version being available in every coffee shop you care to visit. It was invented in the days when chocolate was a luxury, available only to the very rich.

C However, Vienna's stranglehold on the internet chocolate cake market is now under threat from Paris. A well-known French chocolatier has recently joined the battle by designing a 'traveller's chocolate cake' that will be sold from his website.

D Sacher, too, manufactures its own chocolates and keeps the recipes secret, with very good reason. They once employed a foreign trainee chef who spent his time photographing everything. On his return to his home country he opened a café selling the 'original' Sacher torte.

E So he creeps into the kitchen and works through the night. By early next morning he has invented a rectangular chocolate cake made up of layers of hazelnut waffles, filled with chocolate cream, encased in marzipan and topped with milk chocolate icing. The hotel insists that this was the earliest four-sided cake to be made.

F He took his chance and in his boss's absence created a chocolate cake of such complexity that all who consumed it were stunned. His torte was a light chocolate sponge split in two halves and soaked in apricot jam before being topped with a chocolate icing. It was served with whipped cream, as it still is today.

G Now Demel have designed a new chocolate cake, called the Demel torte, for their website, firing another salvo in the chocolate cake war. And these two are not alone in the battle. They have been joined by two new rivals.

Part 3

You are going to read a newspaper article about art. For questions **13–19**, choose the answer (**A, B, C** or **D**) which you think fits best according to the text. Mark your answers **on the separate answer sheet**.

Fake art meets real money

Christophe Petyt has turned the production of exact copies of masterpieces by the world's most famous painters into big business.

Christophe Petyt is sitting in a Paris café, listing the adornments of his private art collection: several Van Goghs, and a comprehensive selection of the better Impressionists. 'I can,' he says quietly, 'really get to know any painting I like, and so can you.' Half an hour later I am sitting in his office with Degas' *The Jockeys* on my lap. If fine art looks good in a gallery, believe me, it feels even better in your hands. Petyt is the world's leading dealer in fake masterpieces, a man whose activities provoke both admiration and exasperation in the higher levels of the art world. Name the painting and for as little as £1,000 he will deliver you a copy so well executed that even the original artist might have been taken in.

Petyt's company employs over eighty painters, each steeped in the style of a particular artist or school. 'We choose them very carefully,' he says. 'They're usually people with very good technique but not much creativity, who are unlikely to make it as artists in their own right. But they love the great works and have real insight into what's gone into them.' Every work is individually commissioned, using new canvases and traditional oil paints, before being artificially aged by a variety of simple but ingenious techniques.

The notional value of the original is not the determining factor, however, when it comes to setting the retail value of Petyt's paintings. This is actually linked to the amount of effort and expertise that has gone into producing the copy. An obscure miniature may therefore cost much more than a bigger, better-known painting by a grand master. The Degas I'm holding looks as though it came off the artist's easel yesterday. Before being sold it has to be aged, and this, so to speak, is the real 'art' of the copy. A few minutes in a hot oven can put years on a canvas, black tea apparently stains it beautifully and new frames can be buried underground, then sprayed with acid.

The view when Petyt started out was that very little of this could be legal. He was pursued through the French courts by museums and by descendants of the artists, with several major French art dealers cheering from the sidelines. This concern was perhaps understandable in a country that has been rocked by numerous art fraud scandals. 'The establishment was suspicious of us,' huffs Petyt, 'but for the wrong reasons, I think. Some people want to keep all the best art for themselves.' He won the case and as the law now stands, the works and signatures of any artist who has been dead for seventy years can be freely copied. The main proviso is that the copy cannot be passed off to dealers as the real thing. To prevent this, every new painting is indelibly marked on the back of the canvas, and as an additional precaution a tiny hidden piece of gold leaf is worked into the paint.

Until he started the business ten years ago, Petyt, a former business-school student, barely knew one artist from another. Then one particular painting by Van Gogh caught his eye. At $10 million, it was well beyond his reach so he came up with the idea of getting an art-student friend to paint him a copy. In an old frame it looked absolutely wonderful, and Petyt began to wonder what market there might be for it. He picked up a coffee-table book of well-known paintings, earmarked a random selection of works and got his friend to knock them off. 'Within a few months I had about twenty good copies,' he says, 'so I organised an exhibition. In two weeks we'd sold the lot, and got commissions for sixty more.' It became clear that a huge and lucrative market existed for faux art.

Petyt's paintings are exhibited away from the traditional art centres – in places with lavish houses in need of equally impressive works of art. Although their owners include rock stars, fashion designers and top businesspeople, they either cannot afford or more likely simply cannot obtain great works of art. Petyt is understandably reluctant to name any of his clients, but says that sometimes even the owner of the original will occasionally commission a copy. 'The best paintings are so valuable,' he explains, 'that it's risky to have them at home and the costs of security and insurance are huge. So some collectors keep the original in a bank vault and hang our copy.'

Is it art? Petyt draws a parallel: 'Take music, for example. Does Celine Dion compose her own tunes – write her own lyrics? She's interpreting someone else's work, but she's still an artist. Classical musicians often try to produce a sound as close as possible to what they think the composer intended. Nobody's suggesting they're anything but artists. With us, maybe, it's the same.'

13 In the first paragraph, the writer indicates that he shares

    A Petyt's enjoyment of the work of a range of painters.
    B the art world's suspicious attitude towards Petyt's activities.
    C the general inability to distinguish copies from real paintings.
    D Petyt's desire to appreciate great works of art at close quarters.

14 What do we learn about the painters employed by Petyt?

    A They have been specially trained in the techniques of forgery.
    B They were chosen because of the quality of their original work.
    C They have to be versatile in terms of the range of styles they reproduce.
    D They make copies of those paintings which customers specifically request.

15 The price of one of Petyt's paintings tends to depend on

    A the status of the original artist.
    B the time and skill needed to create it.
    C the degree to which it has to be artificially aged.
    D the extent to which the copy truly replicates the original.

16 How does Petyt feel about the attempts to prove that his activities were illegal?

    A He suspects that they were not driven by public-spirited motives.
    B He accepts that they were useful in helping to establish his integrity.
    C He regrets that they gained the support of other art dealers in France.
    D He respects the right of the real artists' families to protect their interests.

17 As a result of the court case he won, Petyt

    A no longer reproduces fake signatures on paintings he sells.
    B has been able to copy the work of more contemporary artists.
    C is obliged to make sure his products can be identified as copies.
    D has agreed not to market his products through certain channels.

18 What do we learn about the way Petyt selected the paintings that would appear in his exhibition?

    A They needed to be ones that could be reproduced quickly.
    B It was not something that he put a great deal of thought into.
    C They had to be pictures that would appeal to the buying public.
    D He did some research into the work of artists he'd always admired.

19 What is implied about the majority of Petyt's customers?

    A They have little genuine interest in contemporary art.
    B They regard works of art as a lifestyle accessory.
    C They may buy the paintings purely as a form of financial investment.
    D They are wealthy enough to buy the original works of art if they wanted.

Part 4

You are going to read an article about leisure clothes. For questions **20–34**, choose from the sections (**A–E**). The sections may be chosen more than once.

Mark your answers **on the separate answer sheet**.

Note: When more than one answer is required, these may be given **in any order**.

Which section mentions the following?

a creation by one company that was copied by others	**20**
a company which decided against entering particular sporting markets	**21**
new clothes on the market which are attracting older customers	**22**
the way a company promoted itself in its early days	**23**
an advantage that the current materials have over those used in the past	**24**
the fact that the marine clothing market is not as large as one might expect	**25**
a company's products being popular in unexpected markets	**26** **27**
a company which successfully expanded its range of outdoor wear	**28**
the fact that sporting clothes have become an essential part of the general clothing industry	**29** **30**
a company which opted not to compete in the fashion market	**31** **32**
resistance to a change in approach	**33**
the kind of information that companies provide for potential customers	**34**

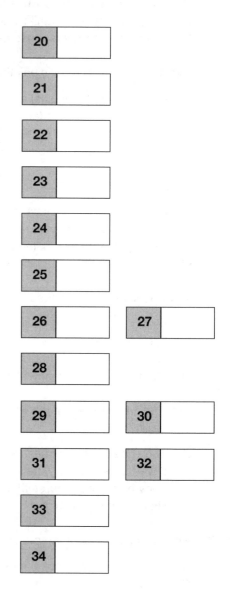

OFFSHORE VESTMENTS

Initially designed for yachtsmen, marine clothing then unwittingly took the male fashion scene by storm.
Now this modern leisurewear is becoming increasingly popular. Keith Wheatley reports.

A

When American rap star M.C. Hammer appeared in a video draped in a baggy, high-tech Helly Hansen sailing jacket, he started a trend in nightclub fashion. The singer was more likely to have stepped from a limousine than a racing yacht (Helly Hansens were worn by the crews in the Whitbread Round the World Race) but the nautical origin of the clothes did not deter the fans. Across the US, sales began to soar – but in unlikely urban retail outlets rather than marine sales centres. Suddenly male fashion was all at sea. 'There's an element of fashion, especially with active role models, like British solo yachtsman Pete Goss,' says Sarah Woodhead, editor of the trade fashion magazine *Menswear*. 'But this marine-look, high-tech clothing thing has moved from a trend to a staple in the male clothing industry, and that's true right across Europe. It's also bringing in a new, more mature, fashion customer.'

B

Brand names that were once synonymous with yachts and epic voyages are now cropping up in every High Street. Musto, probably the biggest company in the sector, was founded some 30 years ago by Keith Musto, winner of a dinghy silver medal at the 1964 Olympic Games. The first sailing clothes were born out of Musto's frustration with the inadequate clothing then available. Now the company makes clothes worth £40 million a year. 'We wanted to branch out – away from just sailing gear, which is a smaller business than most people think,' explains Musto's son, Nigel, now marketing director. 'We discounted the fashion route as too dangerous commercially for us. Keeping people warm and dry is what we're good at.' Skiing and mountaineering were ruled out as clothes markets, either because they were too well covered by competitors, or were too small for market growth. But clothing for country pursuits was judged ripe for a vigorous commercial attack. That was over a decade ago and Musto gear now dominates the British equestrian market, from riding trousers to fleece zip-up jackets. 'The biggest barrier we faced was that it is an ultra-traditionalist market, where two factors dominated,' says Nigel Musto. 'Firstly, the belief that there was nothing better than the traditional materials simply because they had been used in the family for generations. Secondly, that the older the design of the garment was, the more style points it scored.'

C

The key to penetrating the country clothes market was to be the superior performance of modern fabrics: the fact that they are 'breathable' as well as waterproof. The basic principles of breathable fabrics have been known for two decades, and were first developed by an American company, Gore. Gore-Tex is the best known of the breathables and still the most widely used by most manufacturers. Some companies have come up with their own variants but in each case the basic technology remains the same. The manufacturers rejoice in providing pages of diagrams and acres of text which describe in minute detail exactly how each variation on the basic principle works. 'I think this is a key point in its appeal, actually,' says Sarah Woodhead. 'Customers can buy this stuff the way they would a stereo or a car.'

D

'If you'd asked me two years ago whether this surge of interest in high-tech clothing was likely, I'd have laughed,' says Helly Hansen's UK managing director, John Leaver. 'But as a society, we've become brand-besotted, so when kids decide that they want a certain look, they have an instinct for the most powerful brand in that area.' Although Leaver stresses that the company does not deliberately design clothing for the fashion conscious, he is clearly delighted with the additional sales arising from his company's strategic crossover into the mainstream marketplace. Predictably, Helly Hansen is now stocked by major department stores in their trendy leisurewear sections. 'It's provided a growth to our business that would never have been possible from a very restricted marine market,' says Leaver.

E

In 1963 Henri Strzelecki founded his company, Henri Lloyd, and the business is now one of the world's top three in the sector. From the outset, Strzelecki knew the value of publicity and did his utmost to make sure that yachting celebrities such as Sir Francis Chichester were always dressed in his products. Early on, therefore, Henri Lloyd had a secure place in a highly specialised business. Then, in the mid-1980s, huge orders suddenly started pouring in from Italy, hitherto a profitable but very small part of the sailing market. Unknown to the Strzelecki family, a large group of young people in Milan had adopted a fashionable 'uniform' which included a Henri Lloyd jacket, as worn by Sir Francis Chichester, in a distinctive blue with a red, quilted lining. The look spread across Italy, and in the Henri Lloyd factory just outside Manchester, in the north of England, machinists struggled to keep pace with demand.

PAPER 2   WRITING (1 hour 30 minutes)

Part 1

You **must** answer this question. Write your answer in **180–220** words in an appropriate style.

---

1   You are studying at an international college in Ireland. You are a member of the College Film Club, which wants to attract new members. You decide to write an article for the college magazine advertising the club. Other club members have given you ideas on what to include.

Read the information from the college Film Club website together with notes you made on the other members' ideas. Then, **using the information appropriately**, write an article for the college magazine outlining the club's activities and encouraging other students to join.

FILM CLUB

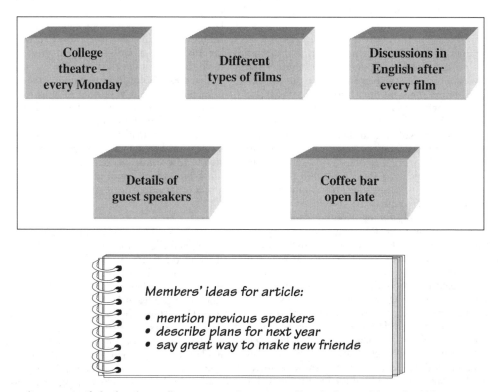

College theatre – every Monday

Different types of films

Discussions in English after every film

Details of guest speakers

Coffee bar open late

Members' ideas for article:

• mention previous speakers
• describe plans for next year
• say great way to make new friends

Now write your **article** for the college magazine, as outlined above. You should use your own words as far as possible.

Part 2

Choose **one** of the following writing tasks. Your answer should follow exactly the instructions given. Write approximately **220–260** words.

---

2   You see the following announcement in an international magazine.

> New TV show – *Hall of Fame*
>
> We are planning a series of documentary programmes on famous people who have made a positive contribution to history.
>
> Who would you nominate from your country?
>
> Write a proposal nominating ONE person from your country, and explaining why this person is important to the history of your country.

Write your **proposal**.

3   An Australian friend is writing a book about traditional festivals and customs around the world. She has asked you to write a contribution to this book, giving her details about *one* festival in your country.

Your contribution should explain the origins of the festival, describe what happens at the festival and say why you think it is still important today.

Write your **contribution** to the book.

4   You see this announcement on the noticeboard of the international college where you are studying.

> ## MAGAZINES AND NEWSPAPERS IN THE COLLEGE LIBRARY
>
> In the library we would like to offer a wider range of reading material to students studying different languages. Please write a report for the library staff recommending **one** newspaper **or** magazine that somebody learning your language would find interesting and helpful. Your report should briefly describe the newspaper or magazine and explain what somebody studying your language could learn about the culture of your country from reading it.

Write your **report**.

5   Answer **one** of the following two questions based on **one** of the titles below.

(a) Kingsley Amis: *Lucky Jim*

You've been asked to write a review of *Lucky Jim* for your college magazine. In your review, explain which character you found most likeable and why, and say whether you would recommend *Lucky Jim* to other students.

Write your **review**.

(b) John Grisham: *The Pelican Brief*

Your teacher has asked you to write an essay on *The Pelican Brief*. In your essay, briefly outline the plot, explain why it is called *The Pelican Brief* and say whether or not you enjoyed the story.

Write your **essay**.

PAPER 3   USE OF ENGLISH (1 hour)

Part 1

For questions **1–12**, read the text below and decide which answer (**A**, **B**, **C** or **D**) best fits each gap. There is an example at the beginning (**0**).

Mark your answers **on the separate answer sheet**.

Example:

0 A inhabited   **B** lived   **C** dwelled   **D** resided

0	A	B	C	D
	▬	▭	▭	▭

The changing earth

Although the earth was formed about 4,500 million years ago, human beings have **(0)** ..... it for less than half a million years. Within this time, population has increased hugely and people have had a vast **(1)** ..... upon the earth. They have long been able to **(2)** ..... the forces of nature to use. Now, with modern technology, they have the power to alter the balance of life on earth.

Reports back from the first astronauts helped dispel the dangerous **(3)** ..... that the world had no boundaries and had limitless resources. **(4)** ..... , ecologists have shown that all forms of life on earth are interconnected, so it **(5)** ..... that all human activity has an effect on the natural environment.

In recent years, people have been putting the environment under stress. As a result, certain **(6)** ..... materials such as timber, water and minerals are beginning to **(7)** ..... short. Pollution and the **(8)** ..... of waste are already critical issues, and the **(9)** ..... of the environment is fast becoming the most pressing problem **(10)** ..... us all. The way we respond to the challenge will have a profound effect on the earth and its life support **(11)** ....

However, despite all these threats there are **(12)** ..... signs. Over the past few decades, the growth in population has been more than matched by food production, indicating that we should be able to feed ourselves for some time yet.

---

1   **A** imprint   **B** indication   **C** impression   **D** impact

2   **A** put   **B** make   **C** place   **D** stand

3   **A** judgement   **B** notion   **C** reflection   **D** concept

4   **A** However   **B** Likewise   **C** Moreover   **D** Otherwise

5   **A** results   **B** follows   **C** complies   **D** develops

6   **A** raw   **B** coarse   **C** crude   **D** rough

7   **A** turn   **B** come   **C** go   **D** run

8   **A** disposal   **B** displacement   **C** dismissal   **D** disposition

9   **A** state   **B** situation   **C** case   **D** circumstance

10 **A** encountering   **B** opposing   **C** meeting   **D** confronting

11 **A** projects   **B** systems   **C** methods   **D** routines

12 **A** stimulating   **B** welcoming   **C** satisfying   **D** reassuring

Part 2

For questions **13–27**, read the text below and think of the word which best fits each gap. Use only **one** word in each gap. There is an example at the beginning **(0)**.

Write your answers **IN CAPITAL LETTERS on the separate answer sheet**.

Example: | **0** | | *O* | *R* | | | | | | | | | | | | | | | | |

Early photography

In the early days of photography, a stand **(0)** ..... some other firm support for the camera was essential. This was because photographic materials were **(13)** ..... insensitive to light that a typical exposure lasted several seconds. The camera **(14)** ..... have to be held still for this time in order to obtain a sharp picture. The subjects also had to be still if their images **(15)** ..... to register properly on the film. Some early street scenes include blurred, transparent, ghostlike images of people **(16)** ..... wandered past while the scene was in the process of **(17)** ..... photographed.

Studio portraits from the late 1800s show people posed rigidly, often leaning against furniture, **(18)** ..... helped them to remain motionless. **(19)** ..... it was important to keep the head still, a support was often provided **(20)** ..... the neck. Bright studio lights, sometimes produced by **(21)** ..... fire to a strip of magnesium or a small pile of magnesium powder, helped **(22)** ..... reducing the required exposure time. These burned with an intensely blue flame that gave the necessary amount of light, **(23)** ..... the smoke was unpleasant and **(24)** ..... was also a risk of fire.

The problems associated **(25)** ..... long exposure were overcome by the introduction of faster, more sensitive photographic plates, and later, roll films. The development of smaller cameras led **(26)** ..... photography becoming a popular hobby. Nowadays, digital cameras have further revolutionised photography, enabling even the **(27)** ..... inexperienced of photographers to produce professional-looking pictures.

Part 3

For questions **28–37**, read the text below. Use the word given in capitals at the end of some of the lines to form a word that fits in the gap **in the same line**. There is an example at the beginning **(0)**.

Write your answers **IN CAPITAL LETTERS on the separate answer sheet**.

Example:

| 0 | F | L | I | G | H | T | | | | | | | | | | | |

The Media Commentator

A live broadcast of any public event, such as a space **(0)** ..... or sporting   **FLY**

occasion, is almost **(28)** ..... accompanied by the thoughts of a   **VARIABLE**

commentator. This may be on television, along with the relevant pictures,

or **(29)** ..... on radio. The technique involved differs between the two media,   **ALTERNATE**

with radio broadcasters needing to be more explicit and **(30)** ..... because   **DESCRIBE**

of the **(31)** ..... of visual information. TV commentators do not need to paint a   **ABSENT**

picture for their audience; instead their various **(32)** ..... should add to the   **OBSERVE**

images that are already there. There will sometimes be silences and pauses

in TV commentary, although these are becoming increasingly rare. Both types

of commentator should try to be informative, but should avoid sounding **(33)** ....   **OPINION**

In sports commentary, **(34)** ..... and impartiality to both sides is vital, but   **FAIR**

spontaneity and **(35)** ..... are valued by those watching or listening. Sports   **ENTHUSE**

commentators usually broadcast live in an essentially unscripted way,

although they may refer to previously prepared materials such as sports

statistics. Because of the **(36)** ..... nature of live events, thorough   **PREDICT**

preparation in advance is vital. The internet has helped enormously with

this aspect of the job. Anyone interested in becoming a commentator

should have excellent organisational skills, the willingness to work

(37) ..... hours and a strong voice.   **REGULAR**

Part 4

For questions **38–42**, think of **one** word only which can be used appropriately in all three sentences. Here is an example **(0)**.

Example:

0 The committee decided to .... the money equally between the two charities.

I can't believe that John and Maggie have decided to .... up after 20 years of marriage.

To serve a watermelon you need to .... it down the centre with a sharp knife.

Example: | **0** | S | P | L | I | T | | | | | | | | | | | | | |

Write **only** the missing word **IN CAPITAL LETTERS on the separate answer sheet**.

---

38 Nikki already had a .... idea of how she wanted her career to develop.

It soon became .... that Paula would not be able to finish the race.

The area in front of the fire exit should be kept .... at all times.

39 It's hard to .... how tall buildings are when you see them from the air.

I have been asked to .... a song-writing competition.

It's a mistake to .... people by appearances alone.

40 'I've got to go now, but I'll try to .... up with you later in the park,' said Jake.

The organisers agreed to .... the costs of clearing up after the pop concert.

The company has failed to .... its targets for the second consecutive year.

41 'We've achieved a great deal in a short .... of time,' said the company director.

Mandy liked most things about her friend's new home but thought that the dining table took up far too much ....

'I've arranged a car parking .... for you,' said the administrator.

42 My neighbour is 96 but is still able to walk without the .... of a stick.

The electronic whiteboard is a wonderful new learning .... for use in the classroom.

Flights carrying .... donated by charity organisations are now arriving in the areas affected by drought every day.

Part 5

For questions **43–50**, complete the second sentence so that it has a similar meaning to the first sentence, using the word given. **Do not change the word given**. You must use between **three** and **six** words, including the word given. Here is an example **(0)**.

Example:

0 Fernanda refused to wear her sister's old dress.

NOT

Fernanda said that .... her sister's old dress.

The gap can be filled with the words 'she would not wear', so you write:

Example: | **0** | SHE WOULD NOT WEAR

Write the missing words **IN CAPITAL LETTERS on the separate answer sheet**.

---

43 We didn't stay long at the party because it was very noisy.

SO

If .... noise, we might have stayed longer at the party.

44 The number of people applying for university grants fell last year.

FALL

There .... number of people applying for university grants last year.

45 Mr Conrad's son is becoming quite well known as an artist.

NAME

Mr Conrad's son is making .... himself as an artist.

Paper 3 Use of English

46 Would you mind helping me carry this heavy box to the car?

GRATEFUL

This box is really heavy so I'd .... help me
carry it to the car.

47 'Excuse me madam, but is this your bag?' the policeman asked.

BELONG

'Excuse me madam, but ....?' the policeman
asked.

48 By the time we got to the sale, every book had been sold.

SINGLE

By the time we got to the sale, there .... book
left.

49 Rosa found it very difficult to persuade her boss to give her a pay rise.

GREAT

Rosa had .... her boss to give her a pay rise.

50 The man claimed that he had been nowhere near the factory at the time of the break-in.

TO

The man claimed not .... near the factory at
the time of the break-in.

PAPER 4 LISTENING (approximately 40 minutes)

Part 1

You will hear three different extracts. For questions **1–6**, choose the answer (**A**, **B** or **C**) which fits best according to what you hear. There are two questions for each extract.

Extract One

You overhear two friends, John and Diane, discussing holiday plans.

1   John thinks Diane's indecision about the holiday is

    A   unreasonable in view of her financial position.

    B   surprising since her holiday is well overdue.

    C   understandable given how much money is involved.

2   How does Diane feel about the prospect of a break from work?

    A   nervous that her boss will regret promoting her

    B   worried that staff will take advantage of her absence

    C   doubtful whether she can clear her backlog of work in time

Extract Two

You overhear two friends discussing a new film.

3   Why has the film been refused a certificate allowing it to be shown to children?

    A   The soundtrack makes it too frightening in places.

    B   The plot is too psychologically complex.

    C   The opening images are too violent.

4   The friends agree that the original story on which the film is based

    A   is written in a rather unusual style.

    B   gives a convincing portrayal of a historical character.

    C   manages to keep the reader in suspense until the end.

Extract Three

You hear an interview with the architect Ingrid Chapman, who is talking about an office building she has recently designed.

5   What does Ingrid think is the best feature of the new building?

   A   the amount of light that comes in

   B   the space she has created for staff interaction

   C   the way each floor has its own facilities

6   What does she suggest companies with outdated office buildings should do?

   A   employ her to design a more modern building

   B   ask staff what kind of workplace they would like

   C   use imagination to improve aspects of the offices

Part 2

You will hear a guide taking a group of visitors around a museum. For questions **7–14**, complete the sentences.

Museum Tour

This museum houses objects collected by the

| | 7 | based in the city. |

It has one of the country's best galleries containing

| | 8 | exhibits. |

The museum's displays of

| *and* | 9 | are closed to visitors at present. |

The section called

| | 10 | is popular with young people. |

The picture galleries contain works on various themes by

| | 11 |

The museum's

| | 12 | needs modernising. |

The guide uses the word

| | 13 | to describe the Rutland Dinosaur's effect on people. |

Polystyrene was used to reconstruct most of the Rutland Dinosaur's

| | 14 |

Part 3

You will hear part of a radio interview in which Harry and Jennifer, two members of an after-work adult drama class, are asked about their reasons for attending the class. For questions **15–20**, choose the answer (**A**, **B**, **C** or **D**) which fits best according to what you hear.

15 How does Jennifer feel about working with strangers in the class?

    A resigned to the need for it
    B doubtful about the value of it
    C relaxed in her attitude towards it
    D excited at the thought of it

16 According to Harry, the improvisation sessions

    A require some careful preparation.
    B enable him to use his imagination.
    C allow him to show his acting talent.
    D encourage him to relate to the group.

17 What does Jennifer say about improvisation?

    A It is important not to make a mistake.
    B It is necessary to be aware of the timing.
    C You should be familiar with the character you invent.
    D You need to be completely involved in the activity.

18 In Jennifer's opinion, playing written parts will

    A be less challenging than improvisation.
    B include research into previous performances.
    C involve guidance from an expert.
    D lead to competition for parts.

19 Jennifer says that the drama classes have taught her how to

    A improve her interaction with people.
    B manage groups of people.
    C develop her natural acting skills.
    D be satisfied with minor achievements.

20 Harry was annoyed because the newcomer to the group

    A interrupted the class by arriving late.
    B was reluctant to participate.
    C seemed unaware of the mood of the group.
    D wasted the tea break with pointless questions.

Part 4

You will hear five short extracts in which British people are talking about living abroad.

TASK ONE

For questions **21–25**, choose from the list **A–H** each speaker's present occupation.

TASK TWO

For questions **26–30**, choose from the list **A–H** the main advantage each speaker mentions about living where they do.

While you listen you must complete both tasks.

A business person	**A** a beautiful language
B pensioner	**B** friendly people
C doctor	**C** luxury accommodation
D farmer	**D** a good climate
E diplomat	**E** interesting challenges
F student	**F** varied sports
G engineer	**G** a high salary
H architect	**H** excellent food

Speaker 1	21
Speaker 2	22
Speaker 3	23
Speaker 4	24
Speaker 5	25

Speaker 1	26
Speaker 2	27
Speaker 3	28
Speaker 4	29
Speaker 5	30

Visual materials for the Speaking test

Why are the flags being used?

What effect might they have on people who see them?

What do the wheels enable people to do?
How important may they be?

How effective might these suggestions be in improving health care?
Which two suggestions would benefit the local community most?

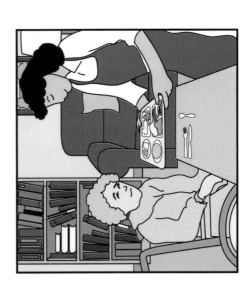

Why do children enjoy games like these?

What might children learn from playing them?

What feelings are being expressed?
What might have made the people feel like this?

How great might the demand be for these improvements?
Which would be the most, and which the least, effective in attracting more passengers?

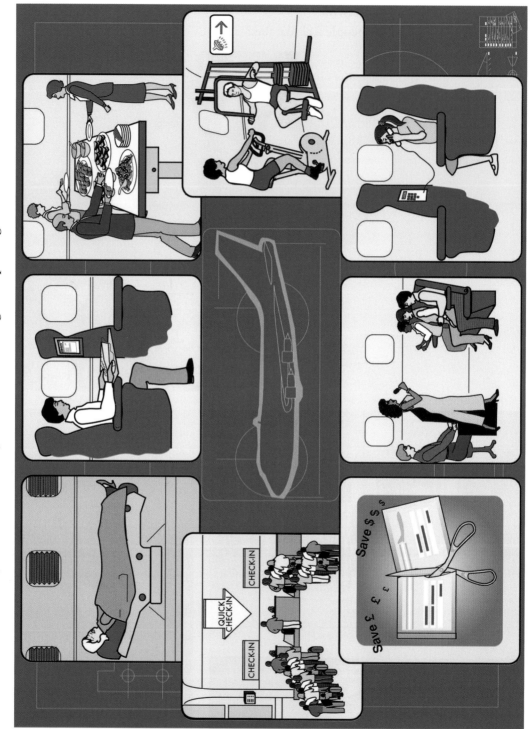

How practical is it to store things in these ways?
How easy might it be for people to find what they are looking for?

What kind of customer might they attract?

What might be the advantage of shopping in these places?

How can the weather conditions affect people's lives?
Which two kinds of weather conditions could have the most harmful effects?

What aspects of the past do the photographs show?

How might the people be feeling as they look back on the past?

What might have caused these events?

How could they have been prevented?

How might these activities help people escape from the pressures of everyday life?
Which two would have the most lasting benefit?

PAPER 5   SPEAKING (15 minutes)

There are two examiners. One (the interlocutor) conducts the test, providing you with the necessary materials and explaining what you have to do. The other examiner (the assessor) is introduced to you, but then takes no further part in the interaction.

Part 1 (3 minutes)

The interlocutor first asks you and your partner a few questions. The interlocutor asks candidates for some information about themselves, then widens the scope of the questions by asking about, e.g. candidates' leisure activities, studies, travel and daily life. Candidates are expected to respond to the interlocutor's questions, and listen to what their partner has to say.

Part 2 (a one-minute long turn for each candidate, plus 30-second response from the second candidate)

You are each given the opportunity to talk for about a minute, and to comment briefly after your partner has spoken.

The interlocutor gives you a set of pictures and asks you to talk about them for about one minute. It is important to listen carefully to the interlocutor's instructions. The interlocutor then asks your partner a question about your pictures and your partner responds briefly.

You are then given another set of pictures to look at. Your partner talks about these pictures for about one minute. This time the interlocutor asks you a question about your partner's pictures and you respond briefly.

Part 3 (approximately 4 minutes)

In this part of the test you and your partner are asked to talk together. The interlocutor places a new set of pictures on the table between you. This stimulus provides the basis for a discussion.

The interlocutor explains what you have to do.

Part 4 (approximately 4 minutes)

The interlocutor asks some further questions, which leads to a more general discussion of what you have talked about in Part 3. You may comment on your partner's answers if you wish.

Test 3

PAPER 1   READING (1 hour 15 minutes)

Part 1

You are going to read three extracts which are all concerned in some way with dance. For questions **1–6**, choose the answer (**A**, **B**, **C** or **D**) which you think fits best according to the text. Mark your answers **on the separate answer sheet**.

A choreographer's diary

May saw the premiere of my first full-length narrative ballet – *The Ballet Shoes* – for the London Children's Ballet. I have to say, I was wondering if it was going to come off or not. In the studio the week before, I could see nothing exciting – no action. The dancing was coming along okay but the children's acting seemed stiff and contrived. Well, that's one lesson I've learned – don't worry about children performing. Or at least, not until they reach a shy/awkward adolescence where self-criticism overrides any fun. No, as soon as this lot set foot on the stage, the dance floor might as well have been a trampoline. They were well and truly stage-struck, jumping and whirling around like crazy.

Thanks to the efforts of too-many-people-to-mention, the premiere went according to plan. I wasn't really able to watch it objectively that night but when I came back to see the last show – the seventh performance in four days, I was actually smiling along with most of the audience. I have to admit to having watery eyes and after twenty-odd Sundays of losing my voice, all was forgotten and I was very proud of 'my children'!

1   What does the writer suggest about the dancers in *The Ballet Shoes*?

    A   They were better actors than dancers.
    B   They were too young to be self-conscious.
    C   They lacked sufficient enthusiasm for ballet.
    D   They learnt ballet techniques amazingly quickly.

2   When watching the last performance of *The Ballet Shoes*, the writer

    A   believed her hard work had been worthwhile.
    B   was surprised by the reaction of the audience.
    C   thought that the show had got better each night.
    D   felt relieved that it was all over.

Opening Night

On Tuesday I went to the opening night of choreographer Ella Winter's new dance show. The work was produced in collaboration with a linguist, a landscape designer, a heart surgeon and an architect. The score, by Antonio Prandini, samples Italian folk songs and their lyrics. There is a minimalist set – white boxes – incorporating a video installation. And there are Winter's eight dancers. The dance involves mechanical-looking repeated-action sequences and a running montage of mimed laughs, whistles, hissing breaths, and twists of the feet. At times, the dancers enact the lyrics of the songs – there are brief fragments of duet – but long sections are difficult to understand or merely banal. Many hands, on this occasion, had not made light work.

At times, I found myself musing on Winter's collaborators. According to Winter, they had given her and her dancers different objectives, and each had brought a method of expression which had not been available to the dancers before. No doubt, but it's hard to view the result, as Winter claims, as something unique in the sphere of contemporary dance. I've been an admiring spectator of Winter as both dancer and choreographer for over 30 years now, but I felt subtly defeated by the show. For me, it seemed a private conversation with a like-minded few. You had to be wearing very strong contemporary-dance goggles to make anything of it.

3   What does the writer say about the show in the first paragraph?

    A   It is unclear which part each collaborator had contributed to.

    B   Too many people were involved in the project.

    C   The dance movements didn't match the music.

    D   The dancers had very different views on the roles they should play.

4   What was the writer's opinion of the show?

    A   It had appeal for a very specific audience.

    B   Each dancer had a unique form of expression.

    C   The choreographer's long experience was evident.

    D   It was very different from other forms of contemporary dance.

A system to notate dance

For at least five centuries attempts have been made to devise a system of notation to record the sequence of movements in dances. Scholars believe that the ancient Egyptians made use of hieroglyphs to do this and that the Romans employed a method of notation for formal gestures. However, the earliest known attempt, recorded in two manuscripts preserved in the Municipal Archives of Cervera, Spain, dates from the second half of the fifteenth century. Since that time, many other systems have been devised. Some were published and achieved a measure of popularity for a while, but almost all, until the present day, fell eventually into disuse.

It is significant that music notation, which opened the way for development in the art of music as we know it today, was first conceived in its modern form in the eleventh century, but was not established as a uniform system till the beginning of the eighteenth. Dance notation got off to a much later start and has undergone a long succession of false attempts. That so many unsuccessful beginnings were made is not surprising. Dance is more complex than music because it exists in space as well as in time and because the body itself is capable of so many simultaneous modes of action. Consequently, the problems of formulating a movement notation that can be easily written and read are numerous.

5 What do we learn about systems to notate movement from the first paragraph?

   A Researchers have different views about how the systems were used.
   B The evidence regarding the use of early systems is unreliable.
   C One system was used in more countries than the others.
   D Some systems have been in use longer than others.

6 Why does the writer make comparisons between music notation and dance notation?

   A to explain why music notation took so long to develop
   B to emphasise the difficulties involved in dance notation
   C to illustrate the similarities between the two forms of notation
   D to describe how notation has affected the development of both art forms

Part 2

You are going to read an extract from a newspaper article about coral reefs. Six paragraphs have been removed from the extract. Choose from the paragraphs **A–G** the one which fits each gap (**7–12**). There is one extra paragraph which you do not need to use. Mark your answers **on the separate answer sheet**.

Reef Encounter

Tropical fish look very colourful to our eyes, but is that how they look to each other? Our reporter Penny Gosh met the man who may have the answer.

If you're snorkelling around a coral reef, you'll see the local marine life in all its carnival colours. But the show clearly isn't just a tourist attraction. For the fish that live on the reef, it's more a matter of life and death. As with any other creature, the survival of a fish species depends on two things – food supplies and breeding success.

7	

Seeing a coral reef in all its glory, you can't help feeling that fish have completely failed to solve this dilemma. The picture, however, only comes into focus when you take the fish's-eye view. For fish, according to Justin Marshall from the Vision, Touch and Hearing Research Centre at the University of Queensland in Brisbane, see things differently.

8	

This means that the carnival looks quite different to the marine life itself. To help him discover exactly how different it looks, Marshall has designed a unique underwater 'spectrophotometer', which analyses the colours of things objectively in terms of their physical reflection. He is also measuring the light available in different micro-habitats.

9	

The general shift towards the blue end of the spectrum in underwater light explains why most nocturnal reef fish, such as the soldierfish, squirrelfish and big-eyes, are mainly red in colour. According to Marshall, some reef fish might see red, in which case they could capitalise on the colour blindness of others and use red markings for private communication. But in most cases, red species are surprisingly inconspicuous.

10	

As any snorkeller will know, lots of reef fish display the sort of colour combinations that suggest camouflage is the last thing on the fish's mind. The bright blues and yellows that are most common, however, are only conspicuous at a certain range. They fade to grey at a distance, because the colours are so close together that they merge.

11	

Wider colour bands will be visible much farther away, of course, but still the fish's-eye view is different from ours. Most recently, Marshall has discovered that fish may see hardly any contrast between the blue of many species, such as tropical angelfish, and the colour of the water around a tranquil reef. More surprisingly, says Marshall, a fish with blue and yellow stripes can be just as well camouflaged, as even this distinct pattern will merge into some backgrounds. When the fish are all together in a shoal, it's hard for a predator to spot where one individual starts and another ends. It's what Marshall calls 'the zebra effect'. If Marshall is correct, then a fish with bold blue and yellow markings can either advertise or hide itself by simply adjusting its behaviour.

12	

In other words, one set of colours can send out very different signals depending on the setting. To complicate things further, most reef fish can vary their colours, whilst it is common for species to change colour from night to day or as they grow older. Colours may even change with a fish's mood – whether it's fighting or fleeing from predators.

A Together with information about the visual sensitivity of individual fish species and their behaviour, this equipment enables him to begin seeing things as fish do. And it is starting to reveal how the showy and the shy can make use of the same bright colours.

B This is because our visual system is a primate one, he says. It's very good at seeing yellows and reds versus greens. However, 30 metres below sea level there is no red light. So fish tend to see blues and ultraviolets well – and to be less sensitive to reds and yellows.

C The striking bands of colour seem to shout 'come and get me' to a potential mate when displayed against a plain background or close up. But put them up against a background of solid contrasting colours and they work on the same principle as the disruptive camouflage used for concealment of military equipment.

D The trouble is that eating and not being eaten both need stealth. Therefore, it is helpful for a fish to blend into the background. To attract a mate, on the other hand, requires a certain flamboyance.

E If this means that fish really can't see the difference, then it looks to him as though they have only two types of receptors for colour. This is a controversial claim, as others have argued that fish have four types of colour receptor.

F During the day, such fish hide in reef crevices. Once there, they may look obvious to human eyes, but to other fish, they blend into the dark background.

G Even in fish which sport fine stripes, such as parrotfish and wrasse, the different shades are distinct for only one metre and certainly no more than five. Beyond this, they too blend into the general sea colour around the reef.

Part 3

You are going to read a newspaper article. For questions **13–19**, choose the answer (**A, B, C** or **D**) which you think fits best according to the text. Mark your answers **on the separate answer sheet**.

Lights, camera, action man

Travel journalist Richard Madden reports on his first trip with a camera crew.

It was books that first captured my imagination about faraway places. TV travelogues always seemed the poor relation to the classic written accounts, although of course the pictures were rather better. And then there was the issue of authenticity. All those pretentious theatrical types dying of thirst in the desert, as if we didn't realise there was a camera crew on hand to cater for their every need. These days programme-makers know that the audience is more sophisticated and the presence of the camera is acknowledged. But can a journey with filming equipment ever be anything other than a cleverly constructed fiction?

I recently got the chance to find out, when I was asked to present two one-hour programmes for an adventure travel series. The project was the brainchild of the production company Trans-Atlantic Films, which wanted the series presented by writers and adventurers, as well as TV professionals. My sole qualification was as a journalist specialising in 'adventure' travel. However, I was thought to have 'on-screen' potential.

The first programme was filmed in Costa Rica. Within 24 hours of my arrival, I realised that this was going to be very different from my usual 'one man and his laptop' expeditions. For a start, there were five of us – director, cameraman, sound recordist, producer and presenter. And then there was the small matter of £100,000 worth of equipment. I soon realised that the director, Peter Macpherson, was a vastly experienced adventure film-maker. In his case, the term 'adventure' meant precisely that. 'Made a film with X,' he would say (normally a famous mountaineer or skier), before describing a death-defying sequence at the top of a glacier in Alaska or hang-gliding off the Angel Falls in Venezuela. Invariably, these reminiscences would end with the words: 'Had a great deal of respect for X. Dead now, sadly . . .'

Part of the brief for the series was to put the presenter in unusual situations and see how he or she coped. One such sequence was the night we spent in the rainforest canopy near the Rincón de la Vieja National Park in Guanacaste province. I don't have a head for heights and would make a poor rock-climber, so my distress is real enough as the camera catches me dangling on a rope some 30 metres up, well short of the canopy platform.

Ironically, it was the presence of the camera, looking down on me from above, that gave me the impetus for the final push to the top. By this time, I'd learnt how 'sequences' were cut together and realised that one last effort was required. I had to struggle to stay coherent while the camera swooped within a few millimetres of my face for my reaction. In the end, it was a magical experience, heightened all the more by the sounds of the forest – a family of howler monkeys in a nearby tree, amplified through the sound recordist's headphones.

Learning how to establish a rapport with the camera is vital and it took me a while to think of it as a friend rather than a judge and jury. The most intimidating moments were when Peter strolled up to me, saying that the light would only be right for another 10 minutes, and that he needed a 'link' from one sequence to another. The brief was simple. It needed to be 30 seconds long, sum up my feelings, be informative, well-structured and, most important of all, riveting to watch. 'Ready to go in about five minutes?' he would say breezily.

I soon discovered that the effect of the camera on what was going on around us was far less intrusive than I had imagined. After a first flurry of curiosity, people usually lost interest and let us get on with our job. We were also flexible enough to be spontaneous. Our trip coincided with an 80 per cent solar eclipse, a rare event anywhere in the world. We were in a village called Santa Elena and captured the whole event on camera. The carnival atmosphere was infectious and made a welcome addition to our shooting schedule.

13 One thing the writer used to dislike about travel programmes on TV was

    A the repetitive nature of many of them.
    B the dull images that they frequently contained.
    C their lack of respect for the intelligence of the viewers.
    D their tendency to copy the style of famous written accounts.

14 What reason is given for the writer becoming involved in making TV travel programmes?

    A other people's belief that he might be suited to appearing on them
    B his own desire to discover whether it was possible to make good ones
    C his own belief that it was natural for him to move from journalism to TV
    D a shortage of writers and adventurers willing to take part in them

15 Shortly after arriving in Costa Rica, the writer became aware that

    A the director had a reputation that was undeserved.
    B he would probably dislike working as part of a team rather than alone.
    C he would probably get on well with the director personally.
    D his role in the filming would be likely to involve real danger.

16 The writer uses the sequence filmed in the National Park as an example of

    A something he had been worried about before any filming started.
    B the sort of challenge that presenters were intended to face in the series.
    C something he was expected to be unable to deal with.
    D the technical difficulties involved in making films in certain places.

17 What does the writer say about the last part of the sequence in the National Park?

    A It taught him a lot about the technical aspects of film-making.
    B He was encouraged to complete it when he looked up at the camera.
    C It changed his whole attitude towards doing dangerous things.
    D He was unable to say anything that made sense at this time.

18 In paragraph six the writer says that he found it particularly difficult to

    A understand what was required of him for a 'link'.
    B change things he was going to do at very short notice.
    C accept certain advice given to him about presenting a film.
    D meet certain demands the director made on him.

19 What does the writer use the experience in Santa Elena as an example of?

    A something they filmed although they had not planned to
    B the friendly way in which they were treated by the local people
    C something they did purely for their own enjoyment
    D the kind of thing that viewers like to see in travel films

Part 4

You are going to read an article about mazes. For questions **20–34**, choose from the sections (**A–E**). The sections may be chosen more than once.

Mark your answers **on the separate answer sheet**.

Which section mentions the following?

a maze whose layout can be varied	20
the fact that making economies can result in a maze not being accessible at all times	21
a maze which is no longer unique	22
the positive advantages of mazes which are not open to everyone	23
an improvement to a particular design	24
the fact that when planting a maze it is easy to exceed the original estimate	25
the suitability of a particular country for cultivating mazes	26
the fact that mazes are pointless in terms of a practical function	27
a maze which reflects the owner's interests	28
a method of finding your way round one maze	29
a body which looks down on mazes	30
the amount of maintenance a maze requires	31
the appeal of mazes to a certain type of mind	32
the fact that mazes do not have a clear path to the centre	33
the fact that people have not been put off by disapproval	34

Mazes

*There are few rules to having your own maze, although getting the design right is one of them.
Then sit back and wait for a few years. Rupert Wright loses himself in the thick of it all.*

A

There is something enduringly eccentric about mazes. They serve no useful purpose, except perhaps to entertain guests you don't want to see for the afternoon. But the English are mad about them. The Royal Horticultural Society rather frowns on mazes, regarding them as a bit of an oddity, but this has not deterred a nation's gardeners. The second largest maze in the world is at Longleat House in Wiltshire; the largest turf maze is at Saffron Walden, Essex. Adrian Fisher, the world's leading maze designer, is English. His firm designs and builds more than 250 a year worldwide, many for private individuals.

B

One of Adrian Fisher's recent creations is for banker Lord Sandberg in the grounds of his estate. The design of the maze celebrates both his passion for cricket and his career in banking. 'I thought it would be fun,' says Lord Sandberg. 'My great-great-grandchildren will be able to run around it and think of me. The only snag is that all the yew trees we planted last year have died, so I am back to square one.' In principle, assuming the plants are not diseased, growing a hedge in a temperate climate such as England's is straightforward. It requires less work and care than a lawn. The hedge will need clipping just once a year. After ten years it will be a decent enough size to get lost in.

C

One Microsoft director is planning to build a maze in the garden of his house in the south of France. Another Microsoft employee is starting work on an elaborate 10-metre-wide decorative pavement maze. Perhaps there is something particularly attractive about mazes to software engineers; we have all experienced that moment when we are stuck in a piece of software and cannot get out. 'One of the beauties of a private maze is that you can have all sorts of things that would not be practical in a public maze, where there are health and safety concerns,' says Adrian Fisher. 'In one maze, I designed a series of angled mirrors disguised in some overhanging arches in order to disorientate people,' he says. 'In another, a three-metre section of hedge rotates on a turntable to change the puzzle design in a few seconds. There is also a cunningly designed wooden bench with hedges behind. Hit the right button and they all roll backwards to reveal a hidden passage to one side.'

D

Mazes have a long and distinguished history. King Minos of Crete instructed Daedalus to build a labyrinth 3,500 years ago. The difference between a labyrinth and a maze is that a labyrinth follows one track towards the middle; a maze is full of trickery, dead ends and wrong turns. The most famous maze in the world is probably the Hampton Court maze in England. There are more than 15 copies of the maze throughout the world. The original was built in 1690. It can be easily penetrated by keeping one's left hand on the wall. This works because the hedge that surrounds the centre is continuously connected to the perimeter hedge. Later, mathematically minded maze makers, such as the Earl of Stanhope, solved this problem by creating 'islands', or gaps in the hedges. Using the Hampton Court technique at Stanhope's best example at Chevening would be pointless. If you keep your left hand on the hedge at Chevening, you end up being spat out again at the beginning.

E

There is something inherently furtive and secretive about a maze. Adrian Fisher is designing a private maze for an individual who plans to give summer parties. Round the first corner guests will be served drinks, then left to their own devices to find their way to the centre, where a band will be playing. Once the party is assembled, various decorative maze gates will be opened. The cost of building a maze is a bit like building a garden: it all depends on size and the number of plants, and if you are not careful, the budget continues to grow. The cost of building hardcore paths adds considerably to the cost, but many people don't bother, preferring just to use the mazes when the conditions underfoot are good. One drawback is the amount of time one has to wait for the hedge to grow. Half the fun of having a maze is watching it grow and knowing that it will be enjoyed for years. Most people turn to an experienced designer. Some, though, decide to design their own mazes, although there are pitfalls: one man who pursued this path watched with satisfaction as the hedge grew beautifully, only to discover that the maze did not work.

PAPER 2   WRITING (1 hour 30 minutes)

Part 1

You **must** answer this question. Write your answer in **180–220** words in an appropriate style.

1   You are the secretary of the student committee at an international college. The Principal is planning an Open Day and has asked you for your comments on a programme of events.

Read the email from the Principal below. Then, **using the information appropriately**, write a report making recommendations and justifying your choices.

From:	principal@cxx.ac.uk
Subject:	Open Day

The Open Day must provide publicity for the college – and be interesting!

What do you think of these ideas:

–   opening speech – me (history of college) OR former student (memories of college life)?
–   canteen open to the public OR international dishes cooked by students?
–   do you think it would be a good idea to give demonstration lessons?
–   could you suggest a suitable student to show visitors round the college?

Now write your **report** for the Principal, as outlined above. You should use your own words as far as possible.

Part 2

Choose **one** of the following writing tasks. Your answer should follow exactly the instructions given.
Write approximately **220–260** words.

2   You read the following announcement in a travel magazine.

TOURISM – IS IT GOOD OR BAD FOR YOUR REGION?

Do you think there should be more or less tourism in your region?
What benefits does the tourist industry bring to your region?
What would be the disadvantages of increased tourism?

Write and tell us your views. We will publish the most interesting articles.

Write your **article**.

3   You see this announcement in an international education magazine.

BEST TEACHER COMPETITION

Everyone remembers their best teacher.

We want you to nominate one of your teachers for our Best Teacher award. Send us your competition
entry, telling us about the best teacher that you have ever had.

Your entry should:
   • describe what the teacher taught you
   • explain how this teacher has influenced your life
   • tell us why this teacher deserves to win the award.

Write your **competition entry**.

4   An international student magazine has asked its readers to send in a review of **two** different
websites that are useful for students. Write a review for the magazine in which you compare
two different websites, including the following points:
• what kind of information each website contains
• how easy each website is to use
• why these sites are useful for students.

Write your **review**.

5   Answer **one** of the following two questions based on **one** of the titles below.
(a) Kingsley Amis: *Lucky Jim*

You see this notice in an international film magazine.

We would like you, our readers, to send in an article recommending a story you think would make a good film and
giving reasons for your opinions.

You decide to write an article recommending *Lucky Jim*.

Write your **article**.

(b) John Grisham: *The Pelican Brief*

As part of your course, your teacher has asked you to write an essay on the importance of
politics to the storyline of *The Pelican Brief*. Outline what part politics plays in the story and
say whether you think these events could happen in real life.

Write your **essay**.

PAPER 3   USE OF ENGLISH (1 hour)

Part 1

For questions **1–12**, read the text below and decide which answer (**A**, **B**, **C** or **D**) best fits each gap. There is an example at the beginning (**0**).

Mark your answers **on the separate answer sheet**.

Example:

0 A primary   **B** dominant   **C** leading   **D** principal

0	A	B	C	D
	—	—	▬	—

Dinosaur discoveries

In the late 1930s, a group of **(0)** ..... American scientists seeking dinosaur fossils made some noteworthy finds. Although one of their expeditions discovered no fossils, it nonetheless **(1)** ..... to be important in terms of the information about dinosaurs it provided. During that historic expedition, which took place along the **(2)** ..... of the Paluxy river in Texas, something extraordinary was revealed: a dinosaur track, clearly **(3)** ..... in the rock. These dinosaur footprints **(4)** ..... their preservation to the salts and mud that covered them and then hardened into rock, before **(5)** ..... to light 100 million years later. Tracks like these are **(6)** ..... to experts. There have been great gaps in scientists' understanding of dinosaur **(7)** ..... , and so such footprints are useful since they provide direct **(8)** ..... of how dinosaurs actually moved. Scientists have used these and other footprints to determine how quickly different species walked, concluding that many kinds of dinosaur must have travelled in **(9)** ..... .

(10) ..... , the tracks of four-legged dinosaurs seem to **(11)** ..... that, in spite of being reptiles, these creatures must have moved in a very similar way to living mammals, such as elephants – a pattern of movement **(12)** ..... from that of most contemporary reptiles, such as crocodiles. This leads to an interesting question. Might existing mammals have more to teach us about the extinct reptiles that once walked the earth?

1 **A** turned   **B** arose   **C** proved   **D** occurred

2 **A** verges   **B** borders   **C** coasts   **D** banks

3 **A** blatant   **B** substantial   **C** distinguishable   **D** ostensible

4 **A** owe   **B** derive   **C** result   **D** thank

5 **A** coming   **B** bringing   **C** appearing   **D** surfacing

6 **A** unique   **B** invaluable   **C** costly   **D** rare

7 **A** action   **B** manners   **C** behaviour   **D** customs

8 **A** basis   **B** support   **C** source   **D** evidence

9 **A** sets   **B** herds   **C** masses   **D** bunches

10 **A** Appropriately   **B** Characteristically   **C** Interestingly   **D** Alternatively

11 **A** point   **B** specify   **C** express   **D** indicate

12 **A** separate   **B** unconnected   **C** detached   **D** distinct

Part 2

For questions **13–27**, read the text below and think of the word which best fits each gap. Use only **one** word in each gap. There is an example at the beginning **(0)**.

Write your answers **IN CAPITAL LETTERS on the separate answer sheet**.

Example: | **0** | O | U | R | | | | | | | | | | | | | | | |

The Best Books

Are there 1,000 books that all of us should read sometime in **(0)** ..... lives? Throughout this year, we will be recommending a collection of books that, when taken **(13)** ..... a whole, will form a library of 1,000 titles that will inspire and satisfy **(14)** ..... kind of reader imaginable. Book lists appear from time to time, often arousing controversy **(15)** ..... being too elitist or too populist. But our list is the result of consultations with bookbuyers and booksellers, people **(16)** ..... know and love books.

Currently, there are well **(17)** ..... a million books in print. Add **(18)** ..... these another 100,000 books published each year and the choice for readers becomes bewildering, **(19)** ..... certain books, both classics and contemporary works, stand out. While our list doesn't identify classics **(20)** ..... the traditional sense, many of the works included **(21)** ..... considered to be classic books. The list aims to make the reader aware of **(22)** ..... is available that is stimulating, rewarding and inspiring. **(23)** ..... else does one learn about a good read other **(24)** ..... by enthusiastic recommendation?

This month we are highlighting fifty books from the area of business and reference. These fifty titles represent the perfect business and reference library for your needs, **(25)** ..... personal or professional. Our selection will help you to expand and enhance **(26)** ..... understanding of today's fast-changing world of business.

Look out for next month's fifty choices, **(27)** ..... will take you a step nearer completion of your 1,000-book library.

Part 3

For questions **28–37**, read the text below. Use the word given in capitals at the end of some of the lines to form a word that fits in the gap **in the same line**. There is an example at the beginning **(0)**.

Write your answers **IN CAPITAL LETTERS on the separate answer sheet**.

Example:

| 0 | I | N | D | E | P | E | N | D | E | N | T | | | | | | | |

Volunteer Project in Lesotho

Lesotho is a small **(0)** ..... nation in the middle of southern Africa. **DEPEND**

The **(28)** ..... of Lesotho lies more than 1,000 metres above sea level. **KING**

With its wild **(29)** ..... landscapes, it is a paradise for nature lovers and **SPOIL**

outdoor **(30)** ..... , and also offers the opportunity for visitors to gain **ENTHUSIASM**

(31) ..... experience of African culture. This is particularly true in the rural **PRACTICE**

areas, where the distinctive and **(32)** ..... traditions of the country are still **COLOUR**

very much alive.

Volunteers are now needed for two related projects for a community-

based organisation in the Maletsunyane gorge, a remote and

spectacular region in the highlands of Lesotho. One project will

involve improving the **(33)** ..... track used by both visitors and locals to **HAZARD**

reach the base of a waterfall in the gorge. For the second project,

volunteers are needed to **(34)** ..... a biodiversity survey of the region. **TAKE**

(35) ..... , much of this area is suffering from overgrazing, hunting and **FORTUNE**

other activities which threaten the **(36)** ..... of the land. **SUSTAIN**

Volunteers will be accommodated in shared rooms. There is a communal

kitchen, and also a chance to experience the local restaurants. Special

dietary **(37)** ..... can be provided for if advance notice is given. **REQUIRE**

Part 4

For questions **38–42**, think of **one** word only which can be used appropriately in all three sentences. Here is an example **(0)**.

Example:

0 The committee decided to .... the money equally between the two charities.

I can't believe that John and Maggie have decided to .... up after 20 years of marriage.

To serve a watermelon you need to .... it down the centre with a sharp knife.

Example: | **0** | S | P | L | I | T | | | | | | | | | | | | | |

Write **only** the missing word **IN CAPITAL LETTERS on the separate answer sheet**.

---

38 The new law means that the tax system will .... in a different way from now on.

Before you .... this machinery, make sure you are wearing the appropriate safety gear.

The surgeon decided not to .... as he felt that the patient's condition would improve without surgery.

39 'I think this would be a good .... at which to take a break,' said the tour guide.

Everyone agreed with Janine's .... that the accounts could have been falsified.

The students felt discouraged because what they were doing didn't seem to have any ....

40 Stella bought the .... for her new living-room curtains in the market and made them up herself.

Jake is going to Italy to get .... for his new historical novel, which will be set in Ancient Rome.

A waterproof .... such as plastic or glass should be used to cover the top of the box.

41 The group .... a new album last month.

The engineer .... the safety catch carefully and then started the machine.

Last year the factory .... five per cent more toxic fumes into the atmosphere.

42 I think that your brother will .... an excellent doctor when he qualifies.

I am afraid I can't .... the meeting on Saturday because I'm busy.

What do you .... of the new manager in the production department?

Part 5

For questions **43–50**, complete the second sentence so that it has a similar meaning to the first sentence, using the word given. **Do not change the word given.** You must use between **three** and **six** words, including the word given. Here is an example **(0)**.

Example:

0 Fernanda refused to wear her sister's old dress.

NOT

Fernanda said that .... her sister's old dress.

The gap can be filled with the words 'she would not wear', so you write:

Example:	**0**	SHE WOULD NOT WEAR

Write the missing words **IN CAPITAL LETTERS on the separate answer sheet**.

___

43 It is essential that this door is kept unlocked.

SHOULD

On no .... locked.

44 It seems unbelievable that this jewellery is almost a thousand years old when it is so well preserved.

HARD

This jewellery is in such good .... believe that it is almost a thousand years old.

45 When it comes to punctuality, Fiona really takes after her mother.

CONCERNED

As ...., Fiona really takes after her mother.

46 You have to be very patient to work as a primary school teacher these days.

DEAL

Working as a primary school teacher calls .... these days.

47 He didn't understand exactly what was wrong until he read Julie's letter.

ONLY

It .... he read Julie's letter that he understood exactly what was wrong.

48 None of the other team members supported Terry's idea.

SUPPORT

Terry's idea met with .... the other members of the team.

49 The region is rich in natural resources.

OFFER

The region has a lot .... terms of natural resources.

50 Because of its price, the book may never become a bestseller.

PREVENT

The price of the book may .... a bestseller.

PAPER 4   LISTENING (approximately 40 minutes)

Part 1

You will hear three different extracts. For questions **1–6**, choose the answer (**A**, **B** or **C**) which fits best according to what you hear. There are two questions for each extract.

Extract One

You hear two colleagues, Eva and Colin, talking about a problem at work.

1   What is Colin's opinion of their new boss?

    A   She fails to consult with colleagues.

    B   She is too keen to establish new working practices.

    C   She has little understanding of the organisation's history.

2   When talking about the problem, Eva is

    A   trying to suggest that it is unimportant.

    B   comparing alternative ways of solving it.

    C   encouraging Colin to take a more positive attitude to it.

Extract Two

You hear an interview with an expert who repairs antique vases.

3   What is the expert doing at the start of the interview?

    A   explaining what can ruin a restoration job

    B   comparing various methods of restoration she uses

    C   describing the difficulties of matching colours during restoration

4   How does the expert feel about leaving visible cracks in the finished vase?

    A   They should be avoided if at all possible.

    B   They are part of the vase's history and should be seen.

    C   They affect the value of the vase rather than its appearance.

Extract Three

On the radio, you hear a visitor talking to a man about the remote island where he lives.

5   The man wants a ferry service between the mainland and the island because

    A   he is keen to develop tourism on the island.

    B   he thinks more young people would come to live on the island.

    C   he feels the island people should not be isolated from modern life.

6   The speakers have different opinions about whether

    A   creating an airport would be advantageous.

    B   building houses on the beach would be advisable.

    C   commercial development would spoil the island's unique nature.

Part 2

You will hear a short radio report about how technology is helping archaeologists who want to learn more about some texts written over 2,000 years ago known as Roman tablets. For questions **7–14**, complete the sentences.

ROMAN TABLETS

The speaker says that an Ancient Roman 'tablet' was about as thick as a present-day

[**7**]

At the site of an old

[**8**], archaeologists discovered about 200 tablets.

Roman soldiers often used tablets when writing letters or documents of a

[**9**] nature.

On one tablet mentioned, the word [**10**] is legible as well as

people's names.

An expert in what's called

[**11**] says that the project is very challenging.

Panels on the tablets were once filled with

[**12**], which provided the writing surface.

Efforts to analyse the original texts using

[**13**] photography were unsuccessful.

New technology is also being applied to other historical texts which were written using

[**14**]

Part 3

You will hear an interview with an architect called Lucy Collett who designs small buildings. For questions **15–20**, choose the answer (**A**, **B**, **C** or **D**) which fits best according to what you hear.

15 Lucy enjoyed building the tree-house because it

    A gave her children somewhere to play.
    B presented an interesting design problem.
    C demonstrated the type of work she does.
    D allowed her to fulfil a childhood ambition.

16 What fascinated Lucy about the historical phone boxes?

    A their international character
    B their luxurious interiors
    C their range of styles
    D the quality of their construction

17 At college, Lucy designed small buildings so that they

    A could be assembled in a shorter time.
    B would comply better with safety rules.
    C would have a wider range of uses.
    D could be built in a simpler style.

18 Lucy got the idea for a folding market stall

    A from her parents.
    B from travelling salesmen.
    C while she was at a trade fair.
    D while she was on an overseas trip.

19 What did Lucy like best about her award-winning design?

    A the shape
    B the display space
    C the decoration
    D the building material

20 The hotel phone booths which Lucy worked on were

    A developed with mobile phone users in mind.
    B designed for countries with relatively few mobile phones.
    C placed at the entrance to the hotel lobby.
    D intended to be the largest feature of the lobby.

Part 4

You will hear five short extracts in which people are talking about problems related to their work.

TASK ONE

For questions **21–25**, choose from the list **A–H** the problem each person encounters.

TASK TWO

For questions **26–30**, choose from the list **A–H** each person's current feeling.

While you listen you must complete both tasks.

	TASK ONE			TASK TWO	
A	a troublesome client		A	keen to bring in changes	
B	poor pay and conditions		B	willing to accept their situation	
C	a difficult colleague		C	sure that things will improve	
D	conflict with management		D	reluctant to make a complaint	
E	a failed project		E	annoyed by messages from colleagues	
F	excessive responsibility		F	aware of their own failings	
G	a lack of promotion		G	miserable in their present job	
H	an inefficient IT system		H	unsure what to do about the problem	

Speaker 1	21		Speaker 1	26
Speaker 2	22		Speaker 2	27
Speaker 3	23		Speaker 3	28
Speaker 4	24		Speaker 4	29
Speaker 5	25		Speaker 5	30

PAPER 5   SPEAKING (15 minutes)

There are two examiners. One (the interlocutor) conducts the test, providing you with the necessary materials and explaining what you have to do. The other examiner (the assessor) is introduced to you, but then takes no further part in the interaction.

Part 1 (3 minutes)

The interlocutor first asks you and your partner a few questions. The interlocutor asks candidates for some information about themselves, then widens the scope of the questions by asking about, e.g. candidates' leisure activities, studies, travel and daily life. Candidates are expected to respond to the interlocutor's questions, and listen to what their partner has to say.

Part 2 (a one-minute 'long turn' for each candidate, plus 30-second response from the second candidate)

You are each given the opportunity to talk for about a minute, and to comment briefly after your partner has spoken.

   The interlocutor gives you a set of pictures and asks you to talk about them for about one minute. It is important to listen carefully to the interlocutor's instructions. The interlocutor then asks your partner a question about your pictures and your partner responds briefly.

   You are then given another set of pictures to look at. Your partner talks about these pictures for about one minute. This time the interlocutor asks you a question about your partner's pictures and you respond briefly.

Part 3 (approximately 4 minutes)

In this part of the test you and your partner are asked to talk together. The interlocutor places a new set of pictures on the table between you. This stimulus provides the basis for a discussion.

   The interlocutor explains what you have to do.

Part 4 (approximately 4 minutes)

The interlocutor asks some further questions, which leads to a more general discussion of what you have talked about in Part 3. You may comment on your partner's answers if you wish.

Test 4

PAPER 1   READING (1 hour 15 minutes)

Part 1

You are going to read three extracts which are all concerned in some way with people living together. For questions **1–6**, choose the answer (**A**, **B**, **C** or **D**) which you think fits best according to the text. Mark your answers **on the separate answer sheet**.

WRITING MY FAMILY MEMOIRS

One problem when writing family histories is knowing how to show people what your family is like. Recording their recollections is the best method, but this is difficult if, like my family, they communicate chiefly through shrugs and raised eyebrows. At one point I thought I had so little material I'd have to give up altogether, but then it dawned on me – my family may be an extreme case, but this is true to a certain extent of all families. Being so familiar with each other, we had learnt to read each other's facial expressions like meteorologists reading a sky.

One of my most potent teenage memories is of taking charge of some sick chickens on our family farm. I built them a special pen, and spent my spare time feeding them. When I told my dad they had all died, I realised he had known this would happen, and that he would not have let my brother, a trainee farmer, persist in such a sentimental illusion. In short, it meant that everyone had realised before I did that I'd never make a farmer. Did my brother, father or mother remember the chickens as a major turning-point, too? No: they did not remember them at all. The only person who did was my sister. She had helped me with them herself – only for me, in my self-absorption, to subsequently forget about her. I soon realised how separate we all are, and that you can only ever tell your own story.

1   In the first paragraph, what does the writer say happened during the course of his research?

   A   He learnt to understand his own family's manner of communication.
   B   He realised his family was not very different from other families.
   C   He found a way of presenting his family to the reading public.
   D   He changed his opinion of the relationships within his family.

2   What is the writer's purpose in recounting the episode about the chickens?

   A   to highlight the differences in personality between the members of his family
   B   to emphasise how attitudes to people and events can change over time
   C   to underline the need to achieve a balanced view of a past occurrence
   D   to demonstrate the subjective nature of people's memories

Living on a commune

Communes have existed since history was first recorded. I grew up on one in the late 1960s, when more than 2,000 were formed in the USA. However, I was never sure what exactly a commune was defined as: only what it was like to live on one. When I left the commune at twelve years old, I was astounded to encounter almost entirely negative views of communes from people in 'mainstream' society.

There are two main types of communes. In the 'anarchistic commune' there is an agreement to reject establishment and organizational worlds. Usually anyone is welcome, members are temporary, and there are no rules. This type of commune usually doesn't last long. For example, the Oregon Farm, a small and short-lived rural commune, emphasized individualism so much so that there were no real guidelines for living – no norms for membership, behaviour or meal times. Members were transient and there were many arguments about who got what and why, and about work. For example, the women felt it was unfair that they had all the housework and childcare responsibilities while the men worked in the fields.

The second type is the 'service commune', in which people pool resources and agree to live a certain way with a motivating philosophy. Membership is more closed, residents must commit to the commune's purpose. This type is socially organized with leaders and rules. Usually this type of commune has a sense of purpose that binds the people within the commune together toward a common goal.

3   What does the writer imply about communes in the first paragraph?

  A   They are better than life in mainstream society.
  B   They are generally misunderstood.
  C   They are ideal places for children.
  D   They are of very little value.

4   What is the main difference the writer identifies between 'anarchistic' and 'service' communes?

  A   the people who join the commune
  B   the division of work on the commune
  C   the reason for setting up the commune
  D   the areas of conflict within the commune

Interviewing Londoners

A common ingredient in all the memories which people shared with me, as they looked back and thought about how they remembered their lives in a poor district of London in the 1930s and 40s, was a real sense of loss for the time when 'we were all one'. A time when you knew all your neighbours; when you sat outside the front door of your house on a kitchen chair during long summer nights chatting and when you helped each other if you had problems, without a second thought. And yet this affection is probably the result of hindsight. When families were living in such close proximity there could have been little opportunity for peace and quiet and even less for privacy.

A striking example of how things have changed in our perception of what we might expect from our local community was seen in the response to my questions about the problems of organising childcare. Women either needed me to explain what I was talking about or they laughed: what need was there for such formalised arrangements when you were part of a large whole which looked out for one another, regardless of whether they were family, friends or simply your next-door neighbour? It wasn't an issue. If a woman worked, and many did – had to – there was always someone to keep an eye out for the kids. That's the way it worked.

5 In the first paragraph, the writer suggests that the people he interviewed

    A were bewildered by the changes in their lives.
    B were disillusioned by family life.
    C were objective in their view of the past.
    D were influenced by a sense of nostalgia.

6 What does the writer imply by saying that the women laughed?

    A They wished that modern arrangements had been available in the 1930s.
    B They identified with the writer's difficulties in finding childcare.
    C They recognised that childcare was a common problem nowadays.
    D They thought that childcare hadn't needed to be organised in the 1930s.

Part 2

You are going to read a newspaper article about a sport. Six paragraphs have been removed from the article. Choose from the paragraphs **A–G** the one which fits each gap (**7–12**). There is one extra paragraph which you do not need to use. Mark your answers **on the separate answer sheet**.

After the Frisbee

It used to be as simple as a bit of fun in the park. Now the Frisbee is back – and this time it's serious business. Simon de Burton reports.

Until recently, the name 'Gucci' was synonymous with expensive handbags and jewellery. Now however, the company's 'G-force' slogan has taken on a whole new meaning, with the introduction of the Gucci Flying Disc, a 20-centimetre diameter circle of semi-flaccid rubber that retails at a smooth £35. This piece of flying fun has literally taken off, leaving Gucci's main stores with a waiting list of customers that grows longer by the day.

7

The difference now is that flying discs are no longer the exclusive domain of college students. Frisbee-throwing has developed into a range of serious sub-sports, from a team game called Ultimate to the unlikely-sounding disc golf, with distance, accuracy, discathon and freestyle Frisbee falling in between.

8

Assistant librarian and disc-throwing fanatic, Brian Dacourt may not quite fit in with the trend in this respect. He is, however, chair of the World Flying Disc Federation and established the first Ultimate world championships in 1986 when just six teams took part. This year there were more than 100. 'It has become a sport played predominantly by professional people,' he says. 'After graduating, they have progressed up the career ladder into powerful jobs before returning to disc sports much more seriously in their free time.'

9

The team version of Frisbee-throwing, the game of Ultimate, is currently enjoyed by around 700 serious players in the UK. Teams are made up of seven players, and the aim of the game is to score goals by passing the disc to a player standing or running inside the opposition's 'end zone'.

10

But Ultimate's rules do not seem to give rise to the dissension, fouls and gamesmanship that some, more prestigious, sports suffer from. A key Ultimate phrase is 'the spirit of the game', which refers to the sport's basic code of conduct. Even at world championship level, referees or linesmen are not needed.

11

The names of Frisbee-related sports are a little more accessible. An individual version of Frisbee-throwing known as 'disc golf' has also grown up, courtesy of financial expert Derek Robins. Robins, Chairman of the British Disc Golf Association, charges just £3 for a round at his course beside the River Avon.

12

Therefore, when players reach the spot on the course where their last throw has landed, they can choose a disc which is the most appropriate one for the next throw – in much the same way that golfers might use a driver from the tee – with the aim of 'holing out' the disc, into an iron basket held up by a chain, in the minimum number of throws.

It is all a far cry from the early days of the Frisbee in the 1870s, when William Russell Frisbie patented his Frisbie pies, in the disc-shaped tins that college students so delighted in throwing to each other, after eating the pies.

A In keeping with this air of gentlemanly camaraderie and enthusiastic innovation, a whole new language has evolved among the game's devotees. Words such as 'force', 'hammer', 'poach', and 'stall' are used to describe the various moves, throws and tactics which the game demands.

B Even a top-class competitor in several of these disciplines would not have to fork out much on equipment compared to other sports. However, the relative cheapness is somewhat at odds with the nature of its devotees: more and more it tends to be high-earning lawyers, stockbrokers, bankers and IT professionals who make up the core of serious players.

C Once in possession of the disc, a player is not allowed to run with it; it has to be worked up the pitch through a series of tactical passes. If it touches the ground or is intercepted, possession passes to the opposition.

D The popularity of this particular brand of disc bears testament to the fact that the fun-filled summers of the 1970s, when Frisbees in parks were a common sight, are enjoying something of a revival.

E But if all this sounds a little too energetic, and you are happy just to chuck a Frisbee to a friend in the park, you will be in good company. Old-style Frisbee fans can still count among their numbers several famous names, including a leading Hollywood movie star and a Formula One driver.

F The rules are similar to those of the famous sport from which it is derived, the obvious difference being the use of flying discs instead of balls and clubs. Players walk the course with a range of five or more special discs which have special edges and are made of denser material than an Ultimate disc, thus allowing them to fly further.

G Indeed, the sport very much reflects the lifestyles of the people who play it. It is all about working together with one's side against the opposition; competitiveness and camaraderie are of the utmost importance.

Part 3

You are going to read a newspaper article. For questions **13–19**, choose the answer (**A**, **B**, **C** or **D**) which you think fits best according to the text. Mark your answers **on the separate answer sheet**.

Travelling sensitively

A tour operator which specialises in environmentally sensitive holidays has banned the use of all cameras. Is this the future of tourism? asks Mark Hodson.

The days of the camera-toting tourist may be numbered. Insensitive travellers are being ordered to stop pointing their cameras and camcorders at reluctant local residents. Tour companies selling expensive trips to remote corners of the world, off the well-trodden path of the average tourist, have become increasingly irritated at the sight of visitors upsetting locals. Now one such operator plans to ban clients from taking any photographic equipment on holidays. Julian Matthews is the director of *Discovery Initiatives*, a company that is working hand-in-hand with other organisations to offer holidays combining high adventure with working on environmental projects. His trips are not cheap; two weeks of white-water rafting and monitoring wildlife in Canada cost several thousand pounds.

Matthews says he is providing 'holidays without guilt', insisting that *Discovery Initiatives* is not a tour operator but an environmental support company. Clients are referred to as 'participants' or 'ambassadors'. 'We see ourselves as the next step on from eco-tourism, which is merely a passive form of sensitive travel – our approach is more proactive.'

However, says Matthews, there is a price to pay. 'I am planning to introduce tours with a total ban on cameras and camcorders because of the damage they do to our relationships with local people. I have seen some horrendous things, such as a group of six tourists arriving at a remote village in the South American jungle, each with a video camera attached to their face. That sort of thing tears me up inside. Would you like somebody to come into your home and take a photo of you cooking? A camera is like a weapon; it puts up a barrier and you lose all the communication that comes through body language, which effectively means that the host communities are denied access to the so-called cross-cultural exchange.'

Matthews started organising environmental holidays after joining a scientific expedition for young people. He subsequently founded *Discovery Expeditions*, which has helped support 13 projects worldwide. With the launch of *Discovery Initiatives*, he is placing a greater emphasis

on adventure and fun, omitting in the brochure all references to scientific research. But his rules of conduct are strict. 'In some parts of the world, for instance, I tell people they should wear long trousers, not shorts, and wear a tie when eating out. It may sound dictatorial, but I find one has a better experience if one is well dressed. I don't understand why people dress down when they go to other countries.'

Matthews' views reflect a growing unease among some tour companies at the increasingly cavalier behaviour of well-heeled tourists. Chris Parrott, of *Journey Latin America*, says: 'We tell our clients that indigenous people are often shy about being photographed, but we certainly don't tell them not to take a camera. If they take pictures without asking, they may find themselves having tomatoes thrown at them.' He also reports that increasing numbers of clients are taking camcorders and pointing them indiscriminately at locals. He says: 'People with camcorders tend to be more intrusive than those with cameras, but there is a payoff – the people they are filming get a tremendous thrill from seeing themselves played back on the viewfinder.'

Crispin Jones, of *Exodus*, the overland truck specialist, says: 'We don't have a policy but, should cameras cause offence, our tour leaders will make it quite clear that they cannot be used. Clients tend to do what they are told.'

Earthwatch, which pioneered the concept of proactive eco-tourism by sending paying volunteers to work on scientific projects around the world, does not ban cameras, but operates strict rules on their use. Ed Wilson, the marketing director of the company, says: 'We try to impress on people the common courtesy of getting permission before using their cameras, and one would hope that every tour operator would do the same. People have to be not only environmentally aware but also culturally aware. Some people use the camera as a barrier; it allows them to distance themselves from the reality of what they see. I would like to see tourists putting their cameras away for once, rather than trying to record everything they see.'

13 In the first paragraph we learn that *Discovery Initiatives*

    A   offers trips that no other tour company offers.
    B   organises trips to places where few tourists go.
    C   has decided to respond to its customers' complaints.
    D   has already succeeded in changing the kind of tourist it attracts.

14 Julian Matthews thinks that the function of the company is to

    A   get people involved in environmental work.
    B   influence the way other tour companies operate.
    C   inform holidaymakers about environmental damage.
    D   co-operate with foreign governments to promote eco-tourism.

15 What does Matthews say in the third paragraph about cameras and camcorders?

    A   They give local people a false impression of holidaymakers.
    B   They discourage holidaymakers from intruding on local people.
    C   They prevent local people from learning about other societies.
    D   They encourage holidaymakers to behave unpredictably.

16 What is Matthews keen for clients to realise?

    A   that certain behaviour may spoil their enjoyment of a trip
    B   that they may find certain local customs rather surprising
    C   that it is likely that they will not be allowed in certain places
    D   that the brochure does not contain all the information they need

17 Which of the following does Chris Parrott believe?

    A   Tourists are unlikely to agree to travel without their cameras.
    B   Local people may react angrily towards tourists who use cameras.
    C   Tourists are becoming more sensitive about their use of cameras.
    D   Camcorders always cause more trouble with local people than cameras.

18 Crispin Jones says that his company

    A   expects its staff to prevent problems over the use of cameras.
    B   seldom encounters problems regarding the use of cameras.
    C   is going to decide on a firm policy regarding the use of cameras.
    D   advises clients about the use of cameras before they leave.

19 Which of the following best summarises the view of *Earthwatch*?

    A   Too many tour operators ignore the problems caused by cameras.
    B   Most tourists realise when they have caused offence to local people.
    C   There are more problems concerning the use of cameras these days.
    D   Cameras enable people to be detached from places they visit.

Part 4

You are going to read an article about over-consumption. For questions **20–34**, choose from the sections (**A–D**). The sections may be chosen more than once.

Mark your answers **on the separate answer sheet**.

Which section mentions the following?

the impact on people of organisations seeking greater efficiency	**20**
an explanation of why happiness is always out of reach	**21**
the fact that people's attitudes towards certain goods have changed over time	**22**
data that has revealed a surprising lack of correlation	**23**
a lack of evidence that people today are more content than they used to be	**24**
the ability of the market to meet people's desire to acquire more goods	**25**
those aspects of life which are neglected in the pursuit of affluence	**26**
the feeling that many people have of being unable to escape the demands of a growth economy	**27**
the countries where it is accepted that people's happiness is reliant on them having ever-increasing levels of material wealth	**28**
the writer's acceptance that there may be something beneficial in the wide availability of certain products	**29**
research that shows the role of certain preconceptions in determining people's responses	**30**
the economic damage that would occur if people stopped aspiring to higher levels of material wealth	**31**
the extent to which maintaining a growth economy requires people to put important areas of their lives at risk	**32**
the suggestion that people are primarily motivated by the need to earn sufficient money to live on	**33**
the way in which business practices can manipulate people's perceptions of what they need	**34**

Over-consumption

*Paul Wachtel asks why economic growth does not automatically
lead to an increased sense of well-being.*

A

In a host of different ways, the economies of the highly industrialised nations of the world have long operated on the assumption that a sense of well-being depends crucially both on the quantity of goods and services available to the population and on the rate at which that quantity is growing. It is easy to understand how such a misconception could hold sway. And yet, there is little indication that people's lives are fuller or happier than those of our parents' or grandparents' generation, who had much 'less'.

Why *is* it that growth has yielded so little in enduring satisfaction? Why do people fail to derive any pleasure from their standard of living when, in fact, they have so much more than the previous generation? To explicate fully the ironies and psychological contradictions of the emphasis on economic growth would require considerably more space than is available here, but to begin with, it must be noted that the entire dynamic of the growth-oriented economies that exist in industrialised countries absolutely *require* dissatisfaction. If people begin to be satisfied with what they have, if they cease to organise their lives around having still more, the economy is in danger of grinding to a halt.

B

The tendency to over-consume results, in part, from advertising. The very purpose of modern advertising is to generate desires; if an ad can make you feel your life is not complete without product X, it has done its job. But ads are not the only source of this phenomenon. Society as a whole is structured to lead people to define their aspirations in terms of products, and new products are constantly being brought out. Moreover, this tendency is exacerbated considerably by another set of psychological factors. A variety of studies have demonstrated that judgements about an experience are shaped very largely by a person's level of expectation. In a growth-oriented society, people's expectations are continually being raised, and so their adaptation level – the level against which they compare new experiences – keeps rising. Only what is above the new standard ever gets noticed. Satisfaction becomes like the horizon; it looks a clear and finite distance away and potentially attainable. But as you approach it, it continually recedes, and after much effort you are no closer than you were when you began.

C

People's expectations being too high is not the only reason for the ambiguous relationship between material goods and a sense of well-being. Many of the ways we gear up for growth actually *undermine* some of the more fundamental sources of satisfaction and well-being, leaving us feeling more insecure and less satisfied than we were before. A number of major studies into sources of happiness concluded that once some minimal income is attained, the amount of money people have matters little in terms of bringing happiness. In other words, above the poverty level, the relationship between income and happiness is remarkably small. What does matter, these studies indicate, are things like love, friendship, being part of a community, being committed to or part of something larger than oneself. But it is precisely these things that a way of life organised around growth and market transactions impairs. The expectations, assumptions, and arrangements by which people in the industrialised world live, lead them to sacrifice a great deal, both individually and collectively, for the sake of perpetuating the economic system.

D

Nowadays, we work too hard as we strive to be able to afford the larger and larger package that defines a standard way of life and we make our working lives less pleasant as we, societally, forget that the workers from whom we extract greater productivity are ourselves, and as more people feel the insecurity of corporate efforts to become 'lean and mean'. And all too often, people attribute all the hours of work not even to the wish to 'make it', but simply to the fact that they must 'make ends meet'. For most people in the West, there is simply the experience of having to keep up with the treadmill. Yet what figures comparing present purchasing power with those prevailing in the 1950s and 1960s (an earlier time of perceived prosperity) show, is that the definition of 'making ends meet' keeps changing. What not too long ago would have defined an upper-middle-class standard of living now feels to most people as 'just making ends meet'. The dishwasher, television set and so forth that once were signs of luxurious living are now perceived to be necessities. Perhaps this is a sign of progress and certainly there *is* something salutary about the fact that we no longer regard as luxuries such items as running water. But as the definition of necessity keeps evolving, we need to bear two things in mind: that the sense of well-being does not increase in the same way and that the earth is groaning under the strain.

PAPER 2 WRITING (1 hour 30 minutes)

Part 1

You **must** answer this question. Write your answer in **180–220** words in an appropriate style.

1 You are studying at an international college. Ms Johnson, the Principal, has asked you to write a proposal on library facilities at the college.

Read Ms Johnson's email below and the notes you have made. Then, **using the information appropriately**, write a proposal to her, explaining why you think the improvements are necessary and outlining how the facilities could be improved.

---

email   Page 1 of 1

From: djohnson@cax.ac.uk
Sent: 15 March 2006
Subject: Library facilities

Can you write a proposal saying what you think we
need to do to improve the library? Money is limited   *too*
so we can't do everything. Can you say which of these   *short!*
things you think are the most important: opening
hours, work space, books, videos, IT, other resources
not   or anything else you can think of.
enough
                                old + boring   *English*
                                                      magazines?

Thanks

Sue Johnson

Now write your **proposal** for Ms Johnson, as outlined above. You should use your own words as far as possible.

Part 2

Choose **one** of the following writing tasks. Your answer should follow exactly the instructions given. Write approximately **220–260** words.

2   You see the following announcement in a telecommunications magazine:

KEEPING IN TOUCH

Are relationships with families and friends and face-to-face contact with people under threat from the increased use of modern technology such as email and mobile phones? Does this technology help to improve real communication or should we get out and meet each other more?

Write and tell us what you think, giving reasons for your views. We will publish the most interesting articles.

Write your **article**.

3   An English-speaking friend is doing some research on public transport around the world and has asked for a contribution from you.

Write a contribution for your friend's research, explaining:
• how important public transport is in your area
• why people are willing or unwilling to use it
• what you think should be done to improve public transport in your area.

Write your **contribution**.

4   You have seen the following advertisement in an international newspaper.

ISLAND ADVENTURE

We are looking for 30 people to take part in an exciting new television programme. If you are chosen, you will all be taken to an island and left for six months with only basic supplies. Have you got the necessary skills to survive? Have you got the right personality to work in a team? Tell us why you want to participate and why you should be chosen.

Write your **letter of application**.

5   Answer **one** of the following two questions based on **one** of the titles below.

(a) Kingsley Amis: *Lucky Jim*

You have been asked to write an essay on Jim Dixon's attitude to work. In your essay, describe how Jim's attitude to work influences his actions and say whether or not you sympathise with his behaviour.

Write your **essay**.

(b) John Grisham: *The Pelican Brief*

Your college magazine has asked you to write an article on the 'bad guys' in *The Pelican Brief*. Your article should describe the role these villains play in the story and say how you think they add to the excitement of the plot.

Write your **article**.

PAPER 3   USE OF ENGLISH (1 hour)

Part 1

For questions **1–12**, read the text below and decide which answer (**A**, **B**, **C** or **D**) best fits each gap. There is an example at the beginning (**0**).

Mark your answers **on the separate answer sheet**.

Example:

0 A scenery   **B** panorama   **C** spectacle   **D** outlook

Example: | **0** | A ▄ | B ▁ | C ▁ | D ▁ |

A guidebook writer

He is five thousand metres up in the Peruvian Andes, with a view of magnificent **(0)** ..... all around. Looking down at the snow-capped mountains **(1)** ..... out below, Peter Hutchison can be **(2)** ..... for thinking that he has the best job in the world. But the **(3)** ..... required to keep it sometimes **(4)** ..... him out. Some days his head **(5)** ....., not from lack of oxygen but from the **(6)** ..... of checking rooms in fifty different hotels.

Peter is in charge of a team of writers working on a series of travel guidebooks. 'Each guidebook contains hundreds of thousands of facts,' he says. 'When I am on a research trip, I sometimes note down eighty points of **(7)** ..... in one day. **(8)** ..... to popular belief, being a travel writer is no holiday! So that others can get the most out of their trips, I have to **(9)** ..... long hours.'

After driving himself hard for a week, Peter **(10)** ..... himself by taking a few days off to **(11)** ..... his own favourite leisure activities, which include scuba-diving and jungle treks. He has an amazingly comprehensive knowledge of South America. 'I'd love to live here permanently,' he says, 'but I have to return to London to chase up the other contributors and make sure the latest book doesn't fall behind **(12)** .... It's due out in October and mustn't be late.'

1 **A** expanding   **B** spreading   **C** broadening   **D** lying

2 **A** mistaken   **B** tolerated   **C** spared   **D** forgiven

3 **A** force   **B** power   **C** effort   **D** attempt

4 **A** wears   **B** brings   **C** works   **D** bears

5 **A** turns   **B** spins   **C** winds   **D** twists

6 **A** strain   **B** affliction   **C** suffering   **D** distress

7 **A** interest   **B** attention   **C** value   **D** attraction

8 **A** Opposite   **B** Contrary   **C** Alternative   **D** Distinct

9 **A** put in   **B** take up   **C** make over   **D** get into

10 **A** celebrates   **B** delights   **C** rewards   **D** praises

11 **A** perform   **B** pursue   **C** maintain   **D** attend

12 **A** timetable   **B** programme   **C** schedule   **D** agenda

Part 2

For questions **13–27**, read the text below and think of the word which best fits each gap. Use only **one** word in each gap. There is an example at the beginning **(0)**.

Write your answers **IN CAPITAL LETTERS on the separate answer sheet.**

Example: | 0 | W | I | T | H | O | U | T | | | | | | | | | | | | |

The history of the cinema

In Britain, the cinema was, **(0)** ..... doubt, the most important form of public commercial entertainment of the twentieth century. Until its popularity was eclipsed in the 1950s by television, cinema enjoyed a period of some fifty years during **(13)** ..... its appeal far exceeded **(14)** ..... of sport or indeed any other commercial leisure activity.

The popularity of the cinema at that time is **(15)** ..... difficult to explain: it was accessible, glamorous and cheap. At **(16)** ..... height, between 1920 and 1950, a very small sum of money **(17)** ..... guarantee a good seat in the cinema. In the 1920s, the usual venue was a small, neighbourhood hall. The audience was drawn from the local area, and could **(18)** ..... some occasions be rather noisy. By the end of the 1930s, **(19)** ..... , the venue was more likely to be in **(20)** ..... of the larger cinemas known as 'picture palaces', which were springing up everywhere in city centres **(21)** ..... accommodate audiences of over two thousand people. **(22)** ..... these establishments, the audiences were expected to be well behaved; the performances were organised just **(23)** ..... military operations, **(24)** ..... uniformed staff on hand to control the queues and usherettes to direct seating arrangements.

These large cinemas attracted **(25)** ..... very mixed audience, although older people were less likely to be cinema-goers than adolescents. As might be expected, people in rural areas were **(26)** ..... immersed in the cinema than were people in towns, simply **(27)** ..... of the greater provision of cinemas in urban areas.

Part 3

For questions **28–37**, read the text below. Use the word given in capitals at the end of some of the lines to form a word that fits in the gap **in the same line**. There is an example at the beginning **(0)**.

Write your answers **IN CAPITAL LETTERS on the separate answer sheet**.

Example:

| 0 | W | E | S | T | E | R | N | | | | | | | | | | | |

How music was written down

The familiar **(0)** ..... system of notation – writing down music using symbols –   **WEST**

has taken thousands of years to develop. In ancient times, elaborate music

was in **(28)** ..... , even though it was never written down. Eventually, however,   **EXIST**

(29) ..... felt the need to record their music, and so the search began   **CIVILISE**

for a system of symbols that could **(30)** ..... denote the exact pitch of the   **RELY**

note to be sung or played, and at the same time tell the **(31)** ..... how long   **PERFORM**

that note should be held.

The ancient Greeks and Romans did this by using their alphabetical letters

in a **(32)** ..... of ways, but the slow development of notation could not keep   **VARY**

pace with **(33)** ..... complex musical developments. The 13th century saw   **INCREASE**

the introduction of colours to represent more complex note values.

With the invention of printing in the 15th century, the writing of notes was

(34) ..... to black and white and the number of lines became fixed at five.   **STANDARD**

By the middle of the 18th century, musical notation had settled down to its

modern usage.

The main **(35)** ..... to this system has been the adoption of expression marks,   **ADD**

which multiplied **(36)** ..... in the 19th century. These convey the composer's   **SIGNIFY**

intentions as regards speed, **(37)** ..... and so on, to the player   **INTENSE**

or singer.

Part 4

For questions **38–42**, think of **one** word only which can be used appropriately in all three sentences. Here is an example **(0)**.

Example:

0 The committee decided to .... the money equally between the two charities.

I can't believe that John and Maggie have decided to .... up after 20 years of marriage.

To serve a watermelon you need to .... it down the centre with a sharp knife.

Example:	**0**	S	P	L	I	T												

Write **only** the missing word **IN CAPITAL LETTERS on the separate answer sheet**.

---

38 Professor Nilsson is one of the leading experts in the .... of genetic research.

The company wanted to purchase the football .... so as to build a new supermarket there.

The walkers were told that they did not have permission to cross the ....

39 The company .... its awards ceremony in March last year.

John .... the ladder firmly while his father painted the window frame.

The file that was destroyed .... some extremely important information.

40 I told the builders that the wall .... rather damp when I touched it.

Dr Rowan .... that it was time for him to retire after fifteen years as chairman.

Karin .... in her bag hoping her wallet was there.

41 There is unlikely to be any .... in the weather this week.

Johann says he is really looking forward to his holiday because he needs a ....

Could you let me have some .... for the parking meter?

42 My father gave me a lift into town and .... me at the railway station.

The estate agent .... the asking price for the house in the hope of a quick sale.

Without any warning a piece of plaster suddenly .... from the ceiling.

Part 5

For questions **43–50**, complete the second sentence so that it has a similar meaning to the first sentence, using the word given. **Do not change the word given.** You must use between **three** and **six** words, including the word given. Here is an example **(0)**.

Example:

0 Fernanda refused to wear her sister's old dress.

NOT

Fernanda said that .... her sister's old dress.

The gap can be filled with the words 'she would not wear', so you write:

Example:	**0**	SHE WOULD NOT WEAR

Write the missing words **IN CAPITAL LETTERS on the separate answer sheet**.

---

43 Sally was all ready to leave the office when her boss asked her to type up a report.

POINT

Sally was .... the office when her boss asked her to type up a report.

44 Mark once worked for an international charity organisation on a voluntary basis.

AS

Mark used .... with an international charity organisation.

45 They plan to repair the bridge this weekend.

SCHEDULED

The repair of the bridge .... place this weekend.

46 If you change any of these arrangements, please be sure to let us know.

NOTIFY

Please ensure that .... change in these arrangements.

47 Most of the problems arose because there was no leadership on the committee.

CAUSED

It was the .... most of the problems on the committee.

48 I didn't realise that she had decided to come to the meeting.

DECISION

I was unaware .... attend the meeting.

49 I'm going to eat less chocolate this year.

DOWN

I'm going to .... of chocolate I eat this year.

50 We got started on the new project immediately.

TIME

We lost .... on the new project.

PAPER 4 LISTENING (approximately 40 minutes)

Part 1

You will hear three different extracts. For questions **1–6**, choose the answer (**A**, **B** or **C**) which fits best according to what you hear. There are two questions for each extract.

Extract One

You hear part of a radio discussion about a football team.

1   What impresses the man about the player called John Elliott?

   A   He is able to keep calm when he gets near the goal area.

   B   He is good at preventing the opponents from scoring.

   C   He can score many goals given the right conditions.

2   What do the two speakers disagree about?

   A   the inflated price paid for the new player

   B   the new player's long-term prospects in the team

   C   the manager's previous mistakes when purchasing players

Extract Two

You hear part of a radio interview with Deanna Carriconde, who has just won a prize for her environmental work in South America.

3   Deanna thinks the underlying cause of the ecosystem changes she mentions is

   A   overfishing by industrial fisheries.

   B   increased local sea temperatures.

   C   growth of predator populations in the area.

4   How do the local fishermen feel about Deanna's work now?

   A   unhappy about sharing their catch with marine creatures she protects

   B   pleased that she has prevented industrial exploitation of anchovies

   C   optimistic about the prospect of catching better quality fish

Extract Three

You hear part of a radio programme about books and reading.

5   Why did the woman read the book she describes?

    A   It was an unexpected gift.

    B   She came across it by chance.

    C   It was recommended to her.

6   What did the book help her to understand?

    A   how strange the world is

    B   how enjoyable stories can be

    C   how she could become a writer

Part 2

You will hear part of a radio programme about cherries, small fruit which grow on trees. For questions **7–14**, complete the sentences.

CHERRIES

The speaker gives the example of

| | **7** | as a crop being replaced by cherries.

To protect young trees from extremes of weather, a

| | **8** | may be used.

Cherries are prone to cracking because there is hardly any

| | **9** | on the skin of the fruit.

The speaker compares the cherry to a | | **10** | when explaining

the effect of rain on the fruit.

Shoppers are advised to purchase cherries which have a

| | **11** | stem and look fresh and tasty.

The traditional view was that cherries need up to

| | **12** | before they produce a useful crop.

The most popular new variety of cherry tree amongst farmers has the name

| | **13** |

While picking cherries, keep a

| | **14** | in your mouth to stop you eating too many.

Part 3

You will hear a radio interview in which an artist called Sophie Axel is talking about her life and career. For questions **15–20**, choose the answer (**A**, **B**, **C** or **D**) which fits best according to what you hear.

15   Sophie illustrates the importance of colour in her life by saying she

   A   has coloured daydreams.
   B   associates letters and colours.
   C   paints people in particular colours.
   D   links colours with days of the week.

16   Sophie's attitude to risk is that her children should be

   A   left to cope with it.
   B   warned about it.
   C   taught how to deal with it.
   D   protected from it.

17   Sophie's mother and aunt use their artistic gifts professionally in the

   A   pictures they paint together.
   B   plays they perform on stage.
   C   objects they help to create.
   D   clothes they design and make.

18   Sophie feels the puppet show she mentions is a good example of

   A   the inspiration she gives to other people.
   B   the admiration she now enjoys.
   C   the expectations she has to live up to.
   D   the assistance she gives the playgroup.

19   Sophie was a failure at art school because she

   A   was not interested in design.
   B   favoured introspective painting.
   C   was very pessimistic.
   D   had a different approach to art.

20   When Sophie had no money to repair her bike, she offered to

   A   take a part-time job.
   B   publicise a national charity.
   C   produce an advertisement.
   D   design posters on commission.

Part 4

You will hear five short extracts in which people are talking about tourism.

TASK ONE

For questions **21–25**, choose from the list **A–H** each speaker's occupation.

TASK TWO

For questions **26–30**, choose from the list **A–H** each speaker's aim for the future.

While you listen you must complete both tasks.

A	travel broadcaster
B	hotel owner
C	guide book publisher
D	tourist board representative
E	environmentalist
F	railway executive
G	manager of a tourist attraction
H	local government official

Speaker 1	21
Speaker 2	22
Speaker 3	23
Speaker 4	24
Speaker 5	25

A	to increase the amount spent by clients
B	to improve our circulation
C	to revive country skills
D	to raise standards overall
E	to restore local transport networks
F	to refurbish the rooms
G	to attract a new type of client
H	to expand tourist accommodation

Speaker 1	26
Speaker 2	27
Speaker 3	28
Speaker 4	29
Speaker 5	30

PAPER 5   SPEAKING (15 minutes)

There are two examiners. One (the interlocutor) conducts the test, providing you with the necessary materials and explaining what you have to do. The other examiner (the assessor) is introduced to you, but then takes no further part in the interaction.

Part 1 (3 minutes)

The interlocutor first asks you and your partner a few questions. The interlocutor asks candidates for some information about themselves, then widens the scope of the questions by asking about, e.g. candidates' leisure activities, studies, travel and daily life. Candidates are expected to respond to the interlocutor's questions, and listen to what their partner has to say.

Part 2 (a one-minute 'long turn' for each candidate, plus 30-second response from the second candidate)

You are each given the opportunity to talk for about a minute, and to comment briefly after your partner has spoken.

The interlocutor gives you a set of pictures and asks you to talk about them for about one minute. It is important to listen carefully to the interlocutor's instructions. The interlocutor then asks your partner a question about your pictures and your partner responds briefly.

You are then given another set of pictures to look at. Your partner talks about these pictures for about one minute. This time the interlocutor asks you a question about your partner's pictures and you respond briefly.

Part 3 (approximately 4 minutes)

In this part of the test you and your partner are asked to talk together. The interlocutor places a new set of pictures on the table between you. This stimulus provides the basis for a discussion.

The interlocutor explains what you have to do.

Part 4 (approximately 4 minutes)

The interlocutor asks some further questions, which leads to a more general discussion of what you have talked about in Part 3. You may comment on your partner's answers if you wish.

UNIVERSITY *of* **CAMBRIDGE**
ESOL Examinations

S A M P L E

Candidate Name
If not already printed, write name
in CAPITALS and complete the
Candidate No. grid (in pencil).

Candidate Signature

Examination Title

Centre

Supervisor:
If the candidate is ABSENT or has WITHDRAWN shade here

Centre No.

Candidate No.

Examination Details

0	0	0	0
1	1	1	1
2	2	2	2
3	3	3	3
4	4	4	4
5	5	5	5
6	6	6	6
7	7	7	7
8	8	8	8
9	9	9	9

Candidate Answer Sheet

Instructions

Use a PENCIL (B or HB).

Mark ONE letter for each question.

For example, if you think B is the right answer to the question, mark your answer sheet like this:

0 A B̲ D E F G H

Rub out any answer you wish to change using an eraser.

1	A B C D E F G H
2	A B C D E F G H
3	A B C D E F G H
4	A B C D E F G H
5	A B C D E F G H
6	A B C D E F G H
7	A B C D E F G H
8	A B C D E F G H
9	A B C D E F G H
10	A B C D E F G H
11	A B C D E F G H
12	A B C D E F G H
13	A B C D E F G H
14	A B C D E F G H
15	A B C D E F G H
16	A B C D E F G H
17	A B C D E F G H
18	A B C D E F G H
19	A B C D E F G H
20	A B C D E F G H

21	A B C D E F G H
22	A B C D E F G H
23	A B C D E F G H
24	A B C D E F G H
25	A B C D E F G H
26	A B C D E F G H
27	A B C D E F G H
28	A B C D E F G H
29	A B C D E F G H
30	A B C D E F G H
31	A B C D E F G H
32	A B C D E F G H
33	A B C D E F G H
34	A B C D E F G H
35	A B C D E F G H
36	A B C D E F G H
37	A B C D E F G H
38	A B C D E F G H
39	A B C D E F G H
40	A B C D E F G H

© UCLES 2008   Photocopiable

111

UNIVERSITY of CAMBRIDGE
ESOL Examinations

SAMPLE

Candidate Name
If not already printed, write name in CAPITALS and complete the Candidate No. grid (in pencil).

Candidate Signature

Examination Title

Centre

Supervisor:
If the candidate is ABSENT or has WITHDRAWN shade here

Centre No.

Candidate No.

Examination Details

0	0	0	0
1	1	1	1
2	2	2	2
3	3	3	3
4	4	4	4
5	5	5	5
6	6	6	6
7	7	7	7
8	8	8	8
9	9	9	9

Instructions

Use a PENCIL (B or HB).
Rub out any answer you wish to change.

Part 1: Mark ONE letter for each question.
For example, if you think B is the right answer to the question, mark your answer sheet like this: 0 A B C D

Parts 2, 3, 4 and **5:** Write your answer clearly in CAPITAL LETTERS.

For Parts 2, 3 and 4, write one letter in each box. 0 E X A M P L E

Candidate Answer Sheet

Part 1

1	A	B	C	D
2	A	B	C	D
3	A	B	C	D
4	A	B	C	D
5	A	B	C	D
6	A	B	C	D
7	A	B	C	D
8	A	B	C	D
9	A	B	C	D
10	A	B	C	D
11	A	B	C	D
12	A	B	C	D

Part 2

		Do not write below here
13		13 1 0 u
14		14 1 0 u
15		15 1 0 u
16		16 1 0 u
17		17 1 0 u
18		18 1 0 u
19		19 1 0 u
20		20 1 0 u
21		21 1 0 u
22		22 1 0 u
23		23 1 0 u
24		24 1 0 u
25		25 1 0 u
26		26 1 0 u
27		27 1 0 u

Continues over →

Part 3

		Do not write below here
28		28 1 0 u
29		29 1 0 u
30		30 1 0 u
31		31 1 0 u
32		32 1 0 u
33		33 1 0 u
34		34 1 0 u
35		35 1 0 u
36		36 1 0 u
37		37 1 0 u

Part 4

		Do not write below here
38		38 1 0 u
39		39 1 0 u
40		40 1 0 u
41		41 1 0 u
42		42 1 0 u

Part 5

		Do not write below here
43		43 2 1 0 u
44		44 2 1 0 u
45		45 2 1 0 u
46		46 2 1 0 u
47		47 2 1 0 u
48		48 2 1 0 u
49		49 2 1 0 u
50		50 2 1 0 u

Sample answer sheet: Paper 4

Part 1

	A	B	C
1	⬚	⬚	⬚
2	⬚	⬚	⬚
3	⬚	⬚	⬚
4	⬚	⬚	⬚
5	⬚	⬚	⬚
6	⬚	⬚	⬚

Part 2 (Remember to write in CAPITAL LETTERS or numbers)

Do not write below here

		1 0 u
7		7 ⬚ ⬚ ⬚
8		8 ⬚ ⬚ ⬚
9		9 ⬚ ⬚ ⬚
10		10 ⬚ ⬚ ⬚
11		11 ⬚ ⬚ ⬚
12		12 ⬚ ⬚ ⬚
13		13 ⬚ ⬚ ⬚
14		14 ⬚ ⬚ ⬚

Part 3

	A	B	C	D
15	⬚	⬚	⬚	⬚
16	⬚	⬚	⬚	⬚
17	⬚	⬚	⬚	⬚
18	⬚	⬚	⬚	⬚
19	⬚	⬚	⬚	⬚
20	⬚	⬚	⬚	⬚

Part 4

	A	B	C	D	E	F	G	H
21	⬚	⬚	⬚	⬚	⬚	⬚	⬚	⬚
22	⬚	⬚	⬚	⬚	⬚	⬚	⬚	⬚
23	⬚	⬚	⬚	⬚	⬚	⬚	⬚	⬚
24	⬚	⬚	⬚	⬚	⬚	⬚	⬚	⬚
25	⬚	⬚	⬚	⬚	⬚	⬚	⬚	⬚
26	⬚	⬚	⬚	⬚	⬚	⬚	⬚	⬚
27	⬚	⬚	⬚	⬚	⬚	⬚	⬚	⬚
28	⬚	⬚	⬚	⬚	⬚	⬚	⬚	⬚
29	⬚	⬚	⬚	⬚	⬚	⬚	⬚	⬚
30	⬚	⬚	⬚	⬚	⬚	⬚	⬚	⬚